SUPERCHARGE
PRODUCTIVITY HABITS

50+ SIMPLE HACKS TO ORGANIZE YOUR TASKS, OVERCOME PROCRASTINATION, INCREASE EFFICIENCY AND WORK SMARTER TO BECOME A TOP PERFORMER

D1351024

John Torrance,

Productivity Coach

Your Free Gift

This book includes a free bonus booklet. All information on how you can quickly secure your free gift can be found at the end of this book. It may only be available for a limited time.

TABLE OF CONTENTS

INTRODUCTION

Your Current Status

Today's workplace or business environment has become ever more demanding and competitive. Irrespective of the type of work you do, your job designation and industry, everything seems to be moving so fast. To add to that, advancements in technology and our near-total dependence on it, and it's easy to see how becoming more productive in today's world is increasingly complicated. In other words, the tools to achieve productivity keep evolving, but the human capacity to meet them appears to be dwindling.

Everyone has the same amount of time: 24 hours a day, 7 days a week, and 365 days a year. However, the ability to get the most out of each day is not common to all. You wake up daily, hurriedly get out of bed, get dressed, and rush off to work. Now, if you are someone who sets daily, weekly, or monthly goals for success, you may actually get some things done. However, most people get bogged down by a myriad of problems and interruptions while at work. Others get into the workplace with personal issues and work-related problems.

In the end, many become demotivated, stressed, and dejected due to the inability to complete the task for each day. The annoying thing is, as the days and weeks go by, the pressure begins to mount. Deadlines are fast approaching, the board meeting is two days away, and the details required for your reports are still on the drawing board. No matter how hard you work, things somehow happen to spiral out of control.

Yes, you are diligent, astute, and hardworking, but everything does not seem to add up for you sometimes. To worsen issues, you still have to take work home in order to meet deadlines. As much as you don't like it, you feel burnt out and are losing steam, yet you cannot stop to catch a breath. The sad news is, the constant running around could be counterproductive to your health, further reducing your productivity levels.

Where You Want to Be

The rules of engagements in the workplace have changed. You must be swift and decisive to stay on top of your game. Two decades ago, it would have been okay to work hard to attain success. However, today's world thrives on the principles of working smarter rather than harder to excel. That's not to say the business environment condones laxity, but due to interactions with human environments, better ways to get tasks done have evolved.

Productivity depends largely on the efficient utilization of your limited time for task optimization. There are time tested tools, productivity systems, and principles to increase your personal effectiveness at work. Working smarter helps channel your energy and resources, leading to increased focus. What you have at last is an adjusted schedule with a better outlook that results in increased productivity and fewer burnouts.

Overall, your focus should be on possessing the ability to identify time wasters in your daily work routine. Next, you want to be in a position to determine how your workflow should proceed, increasing the value of time spent. In the end, you increase your chances of becoming one of the top performers in your industry.

Supercharge Productivity Habits offer you over two decades of my personal experience and knowledge as a productivity coach. It contains time-tested systems and life hacks to help you improve productivity levels considerably. It provides practical steps, principles, and experiences that have shaped my past and helped me to achieve peak performance in all spheres of life.

This book can serve as a personal guide in your journey to self-mastery and improved productivity. Reading *Supercharge Productivity Habits* will help you to:

- Overcome procrastination.

- Increase your efficiency by helping you focus on what's vital to your success.

- Help you develop strategies to work smarter instead of harder.

- Place you on a journey to becoming a top performer in the workplace.

- Take more pleasure in your work.

- Accelerate your learning potential.

- Achieve more from the limited work hours of the day.

- Re-organize work and study time to make you an expert in your field.

- Follow your dreams passionately.

How Realistic Is *Supercharge Productivity Habits?*

Supercharge Productivity Habits contains the principles that have shaped my life for several decades now. Reading these truths will make all the difference in your rise to a more productive life. Most of these principles helped in increasing my productivity by at least 80%. A lot of times, authors and public speakers offer impractical solutions to sound good or to sell an idea. However, this book does not sell hogwash. No, it does not try to build castles in the air by promising unrealistic steps and principles. That's because the bulk of what you will read here revolves around real-life experiences and proven scientific hacks. Other related views are from reliable productivity experts and industry leaders from all walks of life.

Supercharge Productivity Habits: **What's In It for You?**

My recommendations and tips for working smarter and not harder can make you a top performer in your workplace. Consider the purchasing and reading of this book as an investment. As such, the primary aim of this book is to ensure you derive maximum value to boost your productivity measurably.

However, to achieve the best from each chapter and exercise found in this book requires consistency and unrelenting effort. Put into practice the valuable lessons in this book and, over time, you will see immense productivity output. In the end, you have the potential to become one of the top performers in your workplace or industry.

The Promise

If you promise to read carefully with an open mind the information (or hacks, if you will) contained in this book, and put them into practice, I guarantee that within the next few days to four weeks you will see at least a 45% improvement in your productivity level. At the end of one year, your potential and productivity will know no limits!

What to Do Now

To enable you to get the most out of *Supercharge Productivity Habits*, you must create a plan of action on how to read this book. Considering your schedule, set out a specific time during the day to read. As a rule of thumb, the early hours of the day usually offer an excellent opportunity to learn with minimal distractions. Also, determine how many minutes each morning you want to set aside to finish reading this book. You could do a 14 to 40 days challenge to finish this book. It all depends on how fast a reader you are. However, it is not about speed, but about being able to learn and apply the valuable resources found in this book. When reading, I suggest you arm yourself with a pen and a jotter to take down salient points. If you have sticky notes and a board within your room or office, you can stick essential points you do not want to forget to your mirror or door, somewhere within easy view.

Last, but not least, once you learn a new idea, get to work immediately to put it into practice. Please do not wait to finish reading this book before implementing it. Take the learning process one step at a time.

Keep reading now to start supercharging your productivity habits using these 50+ time-tested and actionable steps today.

CHAPTER ONE

DECIDE WHAT YOU WANT

Life is about decision making. You can only rise in life to the extent to which you make up your mind. Therefore, you must decide what you want out of life. Whatever goals you have set for your life or career can only become a reality after you make firm decisions. Life will not bequeath to you what you think you deserve. You only get out of life what you put into it. In most cases, an increase in productivity and any success you will enjoy in life starts in the mind.

Whatever your pursuit in life, work or personal, you first must evaluate your course. Next, you need to set meaningful goals for attaining them. Such goals must also include an action plan for actualizing them. To become more productive, these 6 steps to successful goal setting can help ensure you reach top performance:

1. Belief

Having strong confidence in the process is a vital part of goal setting. If you do not have faith in what you do, then the process of achieving it will wear you out more quickly. Deciding what you want should be predicated on having ample knowledge of what is required.

"Whenever you see a successful business, someone once made a courageous decision."-Peter F. Drucker

Nothing meaningful happens by chance, it takes goal setting and action to see success. A belief in your abilities serves as gasoline for achieving your goals. When you believe in the process, you will strive to own or personalize it. Having faith in the process does not remove the challenges or pitfalls that go with any endeavor. It can, however, help strengthen your resolve to look beyond the temporal setbacks and to focus on what's most important. A firm belief in yourself can help release the energy required to follow the process through. Your thought process can serve as the building blocks to achieving your goals.

Certain lines of thought can only serve as self-limiting. Such self-limiting thoughts are mostly negative thoughts. Positive thoughts and beliefs will help channel your energy toward the attainment of your goals. Once you have decided what you want, having faith in the process makes achieving your goal simpler.

"Happiness is not the absence of problems, it's the ability to deal with them."-Steve Mariboli

"Once you make a decision, the universe conspires to make it happen." -Ralph Waldo Emerson

You are in the best position to inspire yourself to achieve your goals in life, therefore, believe in yourself.

2. Limiting Beliefs

"Every person takes the limits of their own field of vision for the limits of the world."-Arthur Schopenhauer

Certain beliefs are self-limiting thoughts. Limiting beliefs usually send negative vibes that make achieving your personal or work goals impossible.

These limiting thoughts come from your past experiences, environment, and norms. Such limiting beliefs include:

- **Everything or nothing belief**

  The all or nothing belief is an extremist mindset seated on two opposite ends. It's like thinking in black and white without room for a midpoint or balance. In other words, it is either you have everything or you have nothing.

- **Exaggeration belief**

  Persons with an exaggerated belief tend to magnify events or incidences out of proportion. It's okay to think positively and aim for the best, but having an exaggerated belief makes it difficult to set and achieve your work or personal goals.

- **Minimalist belief**

  A minimalist mindset tends to expend energy on small things. It may also involve paying little attention to the intricate details of a particular goal. A minimalist can put off pursuing a goal or consider it as not something significant.

- **Labeling and Mislabeling**

  Labeling is stereotyping yourself based on a past incidence, usually using negative terms. Giving yourself names due to what did or did not occur is another form of labeling. It involves overgeneralizing a situation or experience that could put you in a negative light.

- **Mislabeling**

9

Mislabeling is a form of misrepresentation of yourself. It involves using an inappropriate description of an occurrence or event. Such misrepresentation does not sync adequately with your workplace or personal goals.

- **Hasty Conclusions**

Decisions or judgments made in haste without rational evidence could result in negative outcomes. Making snap judgments based on a person's actions or reactions can lead to inaccurate assumptions. Such assumptions could result in complications in the workplace or in your personal goals.

- **Pessimistic thoughts**

Some lines of thought can only produce negative outcomes. Always seeing the wrong in situations and people can only produce negativity in your personal and work life. People sometimes hold negative feelings and accept them as fact. When this happens, they discredit the truth and choose to believe the negative situations about work, their environment, or themselves. Negative emotional reasoning makes you see a situation as negative because you feel bad about it.

How to Get Rid of Limiting Beliefs

Your belief shapes the person you have become.

**"Learning too soon our limitations, we never learn our powers."-
Mignon McLaughlin**

The only way to make meaningful changes in your life is by making certain adjustments in your belief system. Here is what to do to make the needed change in your belief system:

Self-Reappraisal

Start first by re-appraising your life. In what specific areas do you feel like you are stuck? What aspect of your goal isn't exactly working for you? To get rid of self-limiting beliefs, you need to identify the likely problems in achieving your goals. State these problems in as few sentences as possible.

What Are Your limiting Beliefs?

You need to write down the particular belief systems you perceive as the limiting factors. Identify how each particular belief has prevented you from achieving your goals. For instance, you need to take certain actions to get to the next stage of your goal. However, being pessimistic is limiting you from achieving your personal or work goals. In this case, in order to succeed, you must know the causes of pessimistic feelings and how to deal with them.

Sometimes, a limiting belief can help protect you from certain dangers or actions. They could also become detrimental to achieving another goal. For example, if you are a person who believes in being frugal and must save up as many funds as possible, spending a lot on vacation might appear wasteful. It will take a clear understanding of your goals and the purpose of the vacation to convince such a person to spend more. A vacation trip, for instance, could be a source of relaxation, education, or career pursuit.

Therefore, you could tie spending on vacation to a specific goal to challenge this limiting belief.

"I am not interested in your limiting beliefs; I'm interested in what makes you limitless."-Brendon Burchard

One of the best ways to challenge or get rid of a limiting belief is to find a purpose. When the purpose aligns with your goals, then it becomes easier to push yourself toward attaining it. For a limiting belief, therefore, we must look for ways to overcome them. Certain habits need to change to see the realization of your goals. Does the belief help you achieve your goal at the desired level? If not, then think of ways to get rid of it. Sometimes, the belief might work perfectly for a particular level of your goal. At other stages of your goal, it could become counter-productive. Then, you need to re-appraise the goal and make adjustments.

1. Purpose

"The secret of success is constancy to purpose."-Benjamin Disraeli

John was living the American dream we all look forward to achieving. Immediately after college, he got a job with a high-powered company in the Manhattan area. Within the space of three years, he was promoted to a managerial role. With that position came a car and other benefits, including yearly vacations. It seemed as if John was living the life of his dreams. The next thing for John was to get married and start raising kids.

Eight years down the line and after three kids, it didn't take long before John began feeling overwhelmed. Endless pressure from work and home, unending bills screaming louder than the American dream were too much for John. Feeling frustrated, he decided to take the subway home instead of driving. Boldly written on an electronic billboard on the way home was this commercial from a popular beverage brand: "Find your sparks, make it real!"

Taking a long walk home, John began to think. He examined his work and personal life over the past 8 years. He felt empty inside. *My 9-5 job sucks!* said, John. He wanted more out of life, but couldn't place his hand on what exactly he wanted. As he walked, John kept asking himself the century-long questions most people ask when life seems not to make sense anymore. *What's my spark? Who am I? What's my life really about?*

At one time or the other, we all get to that point in life where the feeling of emptiness steps in. At this point, we begin to ask meaningful questions just begging for answers. Sometimes, the answers to these questions take us on a ride of self-discovery.

"There is no greater agony than bearing an untold story inside."-Maya Angelou

Understanding the reason for setting a goal is a powerful tool. It helps you to keep the goal in focus and align your activities towards attaining that goal. Knowing the reason for your goal will serve as a motivation for achieving it. Finding your purpose in life gives you the springboard to fulfill your life's dream. Your purpose helps define your personal and career choices.

To live a life of fulfillment and enjoy inner peace, you must find out your purpose. Your purpose serves as a compass that guides your life.

"What am I living for and what am I dying for are the same question."-Margaret Atwood

Questions to Avoid in Finding Purpose:

- Can I do it?

- Will it work?

- Who will come to my aid?

- What if I fail?

- What if I lose interest?

- What if I don't make a profit?

- What if I am wrong?

Honest Questions for Finding Your Purpose in Life:

- What would you do even without being paid?

- What exactly do you want?

- What do you find so easy to do?

- What are you passionate about?

- What will you do if you know you can't fail?

- What do you do that makes you come alive?

- What one thing makes you forget to eat or even poop?

- What one thing are you willing to do repeatedly even when people make fun of you?

- What can keep you up so late at night without feeling bored or discouraged?

- What problem do you think you are best suited for in saving the world?

- If you had one year left on earth, how would you use it for? How would you wish to be remembered?

How to Discover Your Purpose in Life

Explore Your Passion

What are you passionate about? The honest questions expressed above provide an easy way to answer the question of life's purpose. Everyone has an innate ability that inspires us to act. There is a deep connection between what you are passionate about and your purpose in life. You cannot create a purpose for yourself, it is already within you.

All you need is to discover your purpose. However, you will not be the best in any discipline because it is in line with your purpose, but you will find it easier to cope and more exciting once it is your life's purpose. Training and development can help hone your skills to make you a top performer in your field.

Therefore, exploring those things that excite you can help you to discover purpose, in finding your sparks. What talents and gifts can you express or explore?

What most people don't understand is that passion is the result of action, not the cause of it.

15

Take action

"The experience is the reward; clarity comes through the process of exploring."-Shannon Kaiser

Once you know what you are passionate about, it's time to take action. It is only in trying things in the area of your passion that you can discover what you are truly good at.

If you spend the bulk of your time thinking about what your purpose should be, you might become frustrated. Finding your purpose is in the doing, not in the asking alone. Relate with others. Utilize those qualities, gifts or talents, even for free. Try out new things. Then you will discover what you love best. The more you utilize your gifts, the more you will discover about you. Over time, your innate abilities become glaring to you.

Do not overthink your purpose—just do it!

Visualizing What You Want

"Visualization is daydreaming with a purpose."-Bo Bennett

As of the early 1990s, the film camera was a popular means of taking photos of your family and friends at events. At the time, film cameras made use of transparent films to capture images in the process, making a 'click-click' sound when you snapped a photo. Before that, however, you needed to insert the film into the appropriate slot. The film was made by popular brands like AGFA, Kodak, and more.

To take a photo, you needed to look into the viewfinder to ensure the subject was at the center. You could also zoom in or out to ensure you were getting the best positioning. Once you had completed about 36 shots, then it would be time to bring out the film. You then took the film to the lab to convert into a negative. The negative was a reel of film for creating a blur expression of the images you snapped. With that, you could identify the best films to print into clear photos.

The journey from having a desire or goal to the actualization of your dreams looks a lot like this process.

"You can't depend **on your eyes when your imagination is out of focus."-Mark Twain**

In other words, visualization involves creating a mental picture of what you want or where you want to be in life. It is a powerful success tool anyone who wants to become a top performer must possess. Everything you wish to accomplish in life first starts as a picture in the mind.

"A picture is worth a thousand words." -Arthur Brisbane

To accomplish your personal or work goals you need adequate focus. At first, the picture will not be clear and appear like a negative. Once you carefully set your goals, just like identifying the right film or exposure to print, then you can work toward actualizing your dreams. Each goal or aspiration has its own specifications to make a beautiful picture. The better you know how to centralize before taking a shot, the better the photo's output. Also, the better the mental picture you create, the better your chance of success.

"Visualization helps our brain send a signal to our body to start behaving in a way consistent with the images in our head."-New York City therapist Kimberly Hershenson

Everyone dreams or creates mental pictures in the mind daily. However, not all mental pictures can produce positive outcomes in your life. Sometimes people use the power of visualization to create a life they don't want. They imagine the worst situations and end up with ugly photos.

"If you can dream it, you can do it." -Walt Disney

Value of Visualization

- It brings your creative sense to life. It won't take long before you start having creative ideas related to your goals.

- Visualization helps channel your mental energy to identify the resources required for achieving your goals.

- Your mental visual picture puts to motion the law of attraction. This law is what causes the people, resources, and situations needed to bring your goals to reality.

- Visualization creates the inner strength or motivation to pursue your dreams.

Tips to Visualizing and Actualizing Your Goals

Know what you want. In clear terms, state what you want. What do you value the most? What is that thing that can give you the most joy? Create a mental blueprint of what your life will look like after achieving this goal.

Describe the Goal in Detail

The secret to describing your goal in detail is to ask yourself: if nothing is stopping you, how would you go about achieving your goal? This has to do with the process of attaining your goal. Create a clear mental photo of what exactly you want. You can write down the process involved in achieving the goals. Act as if you already have all you need to implement the goal when writing.

Create an Emotional Scene of Your Goal

Try to picture the mood, scenes and other scenarios that will accompany the goal once you achieve it. To help inspire you, create a vision board with the relevant images and quotes. Write the short and long term goals associated with the vision.

Get to Work

Start taking small steps daily toward achieving your goals. Don't let the enormity of the goal scare you. Draw an action plan with a timeline to achieve daily, weekly, and monthly goals.

Say Aloud Your Goals

Saying your goals out loud can also help spur creative actions. You can face the mirror or wherever you like and speak your goals, declaring them into life.

Go the Long Hall

Understand that visualizing your goals is not a sprint, but a journey. Along the way, you will face challenges and discouragement from friends and family. But you must learn to stick to your goal, even when it looks like nothing seems to be working.

"All successful men and women are big dreamers. They imagine what their future could be, ideal in every respect, and then they work every day toward their distant vision."-Brian Tracy

Writing Down Your Goal

Everyone can have a dream or carry a mental picture of what they want to achieve in life, but not everyone takes the time to write down their goals in clear terms. Writing down your goals helps you see what it looks like on paper. It becomes easier to re-focus or adjust any aspect that does not make complete sense.

When it has to do with writing down goals, there are three categories of people you will discover. The first set of people do not write down their goals. The second set writes their goals, but without a clear blueprint on how to achieve them. The third set of people write their goals down and set a clear plan of action on how to achieve them. This third group of people does what is known as SMART Goals.

Research shows that less than 20% of people write down their goals in clear terms. One study also states that those who wrote their goals are 1.2 to 1.4 times more likely to achieve them than others.

Why Should You Write Down Your Goals?

Increases Your Chance of Success

Dr. Gail Matthews, a Psychology Professor at Dominican University, California, conducted a study on 270 participants on goal setting. The results showed that people have a 42% higher chance of achieving their goals when they write them down.

Creates Clarity of Goals

Writing down your goals helps you identify in vivid terms what exactly you want. When you write your goals down, you naturally begin to think about the resources you have and the strategies to accomplish them. However, writing down 'I want to be a millionaire when I'm 30 years old' is not enough. You must identify what exactly you will be doing and how you intend on making the millions.

When writing down your goals, you must make sure they are SMART goals. We'll talk more about SMART goals later in this chapter.

It Motivates You to Success

Seeing your goals written down on paper will serve as a motivation to accomplishing them. You can assess how far you are away from accomplishing your goals. You can also identify little successes and celebrate key milestones if you have your goals written down.

Saves You More Time

A well-written and clearly defined goal reduces the number of times spent on guesswork. Once you have your goals written out, you can see the bigger picture better. That way, you can reduce the waste of resources and achieve better time management.

Guidelines for Writing Down Your Goals

So, when it is time to write your goals down, what should you do? Do you scribble down any thought that comes into your head and then refer to it in pursuing your goals? Or, are there laid down principles, values, aspirations, or structures to follow? For instance, here are some guidelines to follow:

- Identify what your work or life goals are.

- Write the goals down using the SMART Goal principles.

- Identify the reasons you want to achieve each goal.

- Make sure you don't have too many goals. In fact, there should be less than 10.

- Write down how you will go about achieving each goal.

"The trouble with not having a goal is that you can spend your life running up and down the field and never score."-Bill Copeland

To succeed with goal setting, you must always review your goals for consistencies. Also, working with an accountability partner will help you know when you've strayed away from it.

Create a Plan of Action

Writing down your goals without a clear plan on how to accomplish them is no different than wishful thinking. To succeed with your goal setting, you must devise a clear order on how you will attain that goal. Without a clear direction, you could become frustrated and stray from your goal.

Tips to Creating a Working Plan of Action

- Break down the goals into smaller tasks.

- Break each task into steps—daily, weekly, and monthly.

- Set a priority for achieving each task.

- Create a milestone for evaluation of success.

- Create a timeline for achieving each aspect of the goal.

- Be specific on what you intend to accomplish at each stage of the goal.

- Carry out regular reviews of your goals, timelines, and tasks to be sure you are in line.

"Shoot for the moon. Even if you miss you'll land among the stars."

-Les Brown

To succeed in goal setting requires a concerted effort. You must take small doable steps daily.

Review Your Goals

Most people only take stock of their goals in the New Year. They make New Year's resolutions that they end up breaking within a week or two. The only way not to lose sight of your goals is to review them regularly. Reviewing your goals is like having a compass to serve as a guide. To increase personal efficiency, you need to review your goals often.

"If you don't know where you are going, you will probably end up somewhere else."-Lawrence J. Peters

Why You Must Review Your Goals Often

- It helps you identify the critical steps in your action plan to ensure consistency with the overall goal.

- Reviewing your goal keeps it fresh in your mind and helps motivate you to further action.

- As you implement your goals, a review of them will help you spot what needs re-adjustments to be efficient.

- You reduce the chances of going off course in implementing your goals.

- It helps you move faster and more consistently.

- You will eliminate the waste of resources when you review your goals. Efforts spent doing the wrong thing will be saved and further increase personal efficiency.

- It is a great way to strengthen your resolve.

"Life is 10% what happens to you and 90% how you react to it."-Charles R. Swindoll

How to Effectively Review Your Life's Goals

Reviewing your goals will be easier to achieve if you have written them down. Only a person without a concrete destination in life will go through life without setting goals. However, to become a top performer in your industry, you must understand how to work your goals. If you already have your goals written the SMART way, then you can review your goals by doing the following:

- Pick a particular time each day to review your weekly goals. Make sure to commit to evaluating key performance index daily in line with your goals. Early hours of the morning work best for some people. It helps put one in top gear to face the day. Evening or bedtime works best for some, as they wake up having a clear idea of what their day will look like. However, we shall discuss more on this in the next chapter on the 5 A.M. Club.

- Evaluate your monthly goals at the end of each month to see how well you have fared.

- Summarize your daily, weekly, and monthly goals into three to ten steps. Putting your goals into smaller steps makes it simple to review them. It also helps you become familiar with the process without making it boring or cumbersome. You can write the steps in your notebook, phone, board, or tools you work with daily.

- At the beginning of each week or month, review the activities of the past week. Take note of the daily, weekly, or monthly tasks completed. Look out for those still in the making and areas where things went wrong. Also, look at better and possible ways of resolving issues.

- Adjust your plans and review the steps to take for the days, weeks, and months ahead.

"If you want to reach a goal, you must 'see the reaching' in your mind."- Zig Ziglar

SMART Goal Setting Techniques

Clarity in goal setting is a major factor in increasing your efficiency. It also helps you to maintain focus. SMART goals go beyond writing a wishlist. They are a way of writing an actionable goal. A SMART goal takes into account the cost of achieving it. George T. Doran invented the SMART Goals method in 1981 for writing management goals and objectives. Key elements in the SMART goal include:

Specific

A SMART goal is one that is spelled out and identified. It is a clear statement about the expected results and the required actions to achieving them. We all have many things demanding our attention daily, but to increase personal or workplace efficiency, we must identify those tasks that will help advance our goals faster. For this reason, make a list of all of your goals and then select those that are critical to advancing your career.

For instance, will it be more likely for you to achieve 25 tasks or 5 daily? How about weekly? It would be best to prioritize each task and narrow-down to 5 to 25 in line with your goals. These five tasks should be the most important ones that will help you to achieve your mid to long-term goals.

Measurable

A SMART goal is one that can be measured. There should be a clear way to judge whether or not you have made progress toward your goal. When setting it, make sure you define how you are going to track success and the key factors you will use to show how you have worked toward achieving your goal.

Achievable

A goal is not a wish list meant for the fairy godmother. It must be something you can put resources together to achieve. For example, a person addicted to smoking cigarettes can overcome the habit. How? By staying away from it. He or she must also avoid friends or places with easy to access drugs or cigarettes. Therefore, to make your goals achievable, you must have the appropriate environment to support that goal. For instance, to cultivate the habit of reading, you could set a target of a number of books to read each month. Then, you take the next steps in selecting relevant themes or books. Lastly, you could pick a schedule for achieving the goal. From there, you place the selection of books for the month on your reading table, in your bag, or where you can easily reach them.

To make the goal achievable, it should be in smaller bits to start, so you avoid becoming overwhelmed. Again, you need to have the tools required to achieve your goals. If not, you have to work out a means to acquire those tools, either by training or seeking help from others.

Realistic

If you are making a wish, then it is okay even if it is a vague one. However, if you want to succeed in your personal or career goals, then it must be realistic. That means it must align with your personal or career goals in the long-term. You also must have access to the needed resources or know-how to get them.

Time-Bound

Every meaningful goal must have a start and end date. A goal without a timeline becomes challenging to measure the extent of success. Breaking down your goals into smaller bits with deadlines for each bit will make it easier to know when each aspect is not moving according to the plan.

Fixing specific timelines also sets the tone on the urgency of the goal. You can read more about how to write SMART Goals and get templates to guide you.

Chapter Summary

- Deciding what you want is the key to achieving your personal and career goals.

- Possessing the right line of thoughts and beliefs will help advance your course better, rather than self-limiting beliefs.

- You are in the best position to motivate yourself to achieve your goals in life.

- Your purpose serves as a compass to achieving your goals. Your purpose should drive your life's decisions and choices.

- One accurate way of finding your purpose is in taking action.

- Creating a mental picture helps make your life goals clearer and easier to accomplish.

- The image you see often can become your reality.

- Visual aids help motivate you toward attaining your goals.

- Writing down your goals increases the chances of accomplishing them faster.

- People who write their goals down focus better and are more likely to achieve them.

- A written goal must include a plan of action to accomplish it.

- A program of action makes it easier to measure growth and success.

- Reviewing your goals helps you to do a proper appraisal to identify issues, failures, achievements, and deviations.

- A SMART goal is one with an expected outcome and the action required to achieve it.

In the next chapter, you will learn about mastering your day so that you can achieve your life's goal. Join the 5 A.M. Club.

CHAPTER TWO

JOIN THE 5 A.M CLUB

Everyone has habits or habitual activities they indulge in. Some are good habits, others are negative habits. However, Robin Sharma says, "Winning starts at your beginning. And your first hours are where the great heroes are made. Own your mornings and you'll master your life." From discussions, highly productive and successful people wake up before 6 A.M. to start their day. Apple CEO Tim Cook, AOL CEO Tim Armstrong, Investor Kevin O'Leary, the CEO of Xerox, Ursula Burns, Twitter, and Square CEO Jack Dorsey, GE CEO Jeff Immelt, all have one thing in common—they all wake up between 3:30 A.M. and 6 A.M. to connect with their day.

For nearly a decade now, I've woken up before 5 A.M. to start my day. And waking up early has had a phenomenal impact on my day and overall life. Habits are things you do often. You do not need any prompting to carry out habitual acts. Why is it important to develop positive habits? Any habit can be learned, negative or positive. Imbibing positive habits will have a lifelong impact on your goals. That's what Robin Sharma's 5 A.M. Club is about. You rise in life to the degree you allow yourself to.

I noticed that I had become very busy and had no time to read, but knew that reading was an important part of my life and a learning tool. When I did a reappraisal of my life's goal, I had to admit this truth. And that's exactly what we all need to do often: reappraise our goals. What is that single activity or skill you could learn that will have a positive impact on your life or finances?

Using Robin Sharma's 20/20/20 rule, I had to work out a way to help me read so I could increase my productivity. The rules state twenty minutes of exercise, twenty minutes of planning and twenty minutes of studying. Well, I plan my day at night before getting into bed. It works better for me as I get up feeling organized, knowing my activities for the new day. I already had a regular schedule for 30 minutes of exercise each morning. Also, it helps to start with exercise, because, once I get into an activity, my day starts fully and I can get distracted. Because of this, I restructured the 20/20/20 for studying, breaking it into 20/20/20 in the morning.

To help me succeed in this challenge, I placed the books for reading in the morning on my reading table. Also, I made sure my alarm clock was set one hour earlier to accommodate the new reading routine for 4:30 A.M. The first day, it was not so pleasant. When the alarm came on, I literally hit the snooze button. By the second ring of the alarm, ten minutes later, I had to drag myself out of bed if I was going to succeed. It takes discipline and a firm decision to excel at any goal.

Day 1 was a total mess as I felt useless and as if I should go back to bed. I barely made it through the first morning as my eyes were heavy, my body felt numb, and I just kept yawning over and over again. Day 2, yes I got out of bed with the first ring of the alarm. I grabbed a cup of coffee and made it to my study. Day 2 was no better than day 1. I slept late, trying to prepare materials for my meeting for the new day. By morning I felt like I should skip day 2, but I still pushed myself to it.

It was after I did my usual daily reflection and planning before retiring for the night that I realized what was amiss. Now, I wake up one hour earlier than I used to and that has taken some time out of my six to seven hours of sleep routine. Since my new wake up time was 5 A.M, I had to push my sleep time to 11 p.m. to strike a balance. Most days, I have to get into bed by 10:30 or 11 P.M.

By day 3, I wasn't so tired like I was day 1 and 2. That improved the quality of the time I spent reading. It also helped me to achieve my goal faster. The power of habit. If you can sustain the desired trait for at least 30 to 40 days, your body will adjust to it.

Robin Sharma's 5 A.M. Club Secrets

Robin Sharma is a renowned Canadian speaker, writer, and success coach with parents from Indian and Kenyan. In his early twenties, Sharma had to deal with the issues most diversity immigrants faced. He desired very much to excel and was willing to put in the extra effort to succeed.

After graduating from law school and becoming a successful lawyer, Sharma wanted more from life. That led to his studying the lives of other successful men and women to understand what makes them tick underneath. The success strategies of these great personalities gave birth to Sharma's books: *Megaliving in 1994, The Monk Who Sold His Ferrari* and his most recent, the *5 A.M. Club.*

Robin Sharma's 5 A.M Club

Robin Sharma has led a simple, but disciplined life based on experiences and training gathered over the decades. That's what gave rise to the 5 A.M. Club. Sharma's personal discipline learned in his 20s helped project him to success and avoid the mistakes made by so many people. Today, he speaks to thousands of people at conferences and other events.

Sharma says that if you can form the habit of rising on or before 5 A.M. every morning to implement the 20/20/20 formula, you can increase your personal productivity. He calls it the 'Victory hour.' If you can judiciously follow the 20/20/20 rule over time, you will become smarter, agile, more self-confident, and experience a boost in creativity.

Sharma's Victory Hour 20/20/20 Formula

To increase personal productivity here is how to utilize your 'Victory Hour':

- Get out of bed by 5 A.M. (You can start by using the traditional alarm clock to help wake you up).

- Exercise and meditate for 20 minutes.

- Strategize and plan your day for 20 minutes.

- Read a book or online material to hone your skills or to learn something new in your field.

How Waking Up By 5 A.M. Can Increase Personal Productivity

Mental Alertness

Waking up early and working your way through the 5 A.M. club will help give you the needed boost to start the day. At such early hours of the day, most people are still asleep; therefore, you are not likely to face distractions. You can concentrate, feel at ease with yourself, and introspect about your goals.

Exercising every morning also has its own mental and physical health benefits for your body. The ability to manage your body weight will give you the feeling of being in charge. Daily exercises not only make you alert but put you in the right mood to face your day. Your body releases chemicals that help you to relax, de-stress, and possibly fight depression. See chapter seven for more details on habits to increase your physical and mental energy.

Expand Your Knowledge Base

Devoting your first few minutes of waking up daily to reading, I must say it is a powerful way to start the day. What one skill or knowledge do you need to acquire to help advance your career or personal goal?

Reading at least 20 minutes every day can impact your life greatly. People who read specific books for a few minutes daily have an increased chance of becoming leaders in their industry.

Reading, just like exercise, improves your cognitive abilities. It increases your learning power and develops your analytical and judgment skills. It is an excellent tool for boosting your intelligence and brainpower. Reading also improves your concentration level.

Feel Rejuvenated and Motivated

Starting your day in top spirit, you can achieve little successes such as exercise, reading, and more. This feeling helps to motivate you for bigger accomplishments all through the day. If you excel at little things, you get this 'I can do it' feeling. It increases your level of optimism and energy all day long. And before you realize it, you are conquering seemingly insurmountable problems.

"Motivation is what gets you started, habits are what keeps you going."- Jim Ryun

Increases Your Self-discipline

Self-discipline is one of the habits of highly successful people. Achieving anything meaningful in your personal or career life will not come cheaply. It takes tenacity, courage, and a strong push to achieve anything great. To wake up early during the cold winter takes resilience. To read daily takes practice and a strong will. To exercise daily for 30 minutes without skipping any day or stopping takes commitment.

To carry out daily tasks that will advance your career or personal growth takes discipline. Doing it at the right time and in the right manner takes even more discipline. Discipline requires both physical and mental strength.

"Watch your thoughts, they become your words; watch your words, they become your actions, watch your actions, they become your habits, watch your habits, they become your character, watch your character, it becomes your destiny." Lao Tzu

10 Early Morning Rituals to Boost Personal and Work Productivity

What habits or traits do you think can help you achieve success in your career or personal life? You must learn the necessary skills for personal productivity. However, before you can become a top performer, here are some traits or habits highly successful people have:

They Get Adequate Sleep

The National Sleep Foundation says adult needs seven to nine hours of sleep daily for a healthy life. To be in the best frame of mind in the morning, you need adequate sleep. Being sleep deprived will reduce your concentration level at work. Therefore, to be at your optimum, you must have a regular sleep time.

Most high achievers get into bed early so they can feel energized and ready for the next day's tasks.

Get Out of Bed Early

Highly efficient people have specific sleeping and waking times. Some of them get out of bed as early as 3:45 A.M. to 4 A.M. Others start their day at either 5 or 6 A.M. At first, you might need the help of an alarm clock to get out of bed early, but with time, your body will adjust to this new routine. As if automated, you will wake up at about the same time daily.

Getting out of bed early each day gives you an excellent time for exercise, spiritual pursuits, mental development, and more.

Meditation Time

Highly efficient people understand the power of reflection. Meditation or reflection time helps you maximize the usage of your brainpower. If you do not know how to start, using a daily meditation app can help you establish a meditation routine. Daily meditation can also reduce stress, fight depression, help you relax, and deal with chronic pain.

Research by Wake Forest Baptist University shows that meditation can reduce pain by 40%. Meanwhile, taking morphine painkillers will achieve 25% pain reduction. According to NPR, meditation can reduce stress and blood pressure. It also increases a person's problem-solving skills, overall wellbeing, career, and personal relationships.

Research for the National Institute of Health and published by the U.S. National Library of Medicine reports that meditation can reduce cognition loss for the aged.

Avoid Coffee Straight From Bed

It's always tempting to gulp down your favorite brand of coffee first thing after waking up. More so, when the weather becomes freezing, the temptation doubles. However, highly successful people understand the importance of resisting the urge for a hot cup of caffeine first thing in the morning. On his way to the office each day, CEO of Twitter and Square, Jack Dorsey, says he stops at the coffee shop for his favorite coffee. However, he begins his day with exercise, then meditation before leaving for the office.

Scientific findings show that consuming caffeine first thing in the morning will block off the energy-boosting benefits. Therefore, your first java cup should come much later, say 9 A.M.

Take Delight In Workouts

I have addressed the importance of exercise and what it does to the body and psyche. Top performers across different industries have a clear understanding of how exercise can help them maintain optimal performance. Exercise helps rejuvenate the body, circulates blood faster, and keeps one mentally alert.

It does not have to be a rigorous activity and can be fun, light exercise. A brisk walk, swimming, dancing, and jogging. Any physical activity that helps your heart beat faster or blood to circulate will do.

They Organize Their Schedule for the Day

Yes, some powerful corporate individuals employ personal assistants to run their schedules, but highly successful people also check through and organize their schedules personally. Organizing your schedule helps to ensure your day goes as planned with fewer hiccups.

Once they prioritize the day's activities, it helps successful people to work in an orderly manner. They have a clear idea of what it is they want to achieve by the end of each day. Even when there are setbacks or interruptions, it becomes easier to track their progress.

Highly successful people organize their schedules to help them devote their most productive time of the day to their most critical task in line with their goals.

Healthy Eating Habits

Breakfast is one of the most important meals of the day. And high flyers understand the importance of eating breakfast for productivity's sake. Breakfast comes after the long fast from your last meal yesterday. Therefore, your body needs the meal to serve as fuel. You will feel a lot better eating and eating right to face the tasks of the day.

Sometimes, you get excited or do not feel the need to eat breakfast. So, you feel tempted to skip the first meal of the day. However, like Richard Branson, CEO of Virgin Group, says, you can eat something light to start the day. Fruits, whole grains, carbohydrates, proteins, and more should be ideal.

Dress Simply

Highly successful people tend to spend less time trying to figure out what to wear each day. They would rather invest the energy on more productive things than create mental stress from clothing. What most successful people do is to create a selection of simple clothing. They wear exciting color blends, sneakers, or easy footwear, as well as mix-and-match outfits. With such great combinations, it makes it easy for these CEOs and busy executives to pick their clothing daily. For instance, Facebook CEO Mark Zuckerberg told the Independent that he wears a particular collection of clothing to simplify his dressing and conserve his mental energy for the day's job.

Mark is popular for his jeans, gray t-shirt and sweatshirt. Other tech billionaires wear simple clothing too. Steve Jobs wore a turtleneck sweater and black jeans often. Snap CEO Evan Spiegel wears a white v-neck t-shirt with black jeans and white sneakers. Sundar Pichai, Google CEO prefers a simple track jacket, jeans and sneakers, Jack Dorsey wears his regular jeans, black round neck t-shirt, and sneakers. Looking smart doesn't have to cost very much or take all the time in the world. However, wear appropriate clothing and appear smart to boost your confidence.

Create a Work Pattern

How best to tackle the tasks of the day remains an issue in the front burner, eliciting varied opinions. While some people start the day by attending to smaller tasks like reading emails, letters, etc., others begin with the most challenging projects and then narrow them down. However, whichever works for you, ensure the first one hour of work is a productive one.

After prioritizing the tasks for the day, I start my work schedule with smaller jobs that do not require so much time to accomplish. However, these tasks can impact my bottom line for the day. Activities like checking my emails, letters, other messages, and more, usually come up when sorting the things I need to commence work. Once I have the documents and tools I need on my table, I launch into the more significant tasks of the day.

The more significant tasks might take another 3 to 5 hours or more to clear from my table. During work hours, I only read and respond to work-related emails at a specific time. However, during my social or casual breaks, I take out time to check emails and social media feeds when I need to take my mind off work for a few minutes.

Multitask

Although research shows that multitasking reduces efficiency levels at work, successful people exploit it in their routines. For instance, the New York Times reports that Microsoft Founder Bill Gates watches DVDs while exercising to continue learning. Personally, the restroom is a desirable place for reflecting or reading for me. It helps me to relax, reflect on past activities, and come up with great ideas on how to resolve some life issues. I not only empty my bowels but gain fresh insight into a task at hand.

Tips for Getting the Best From Sharma's 5 A.M. Club

- To get adequate sleep at night, try to switch off all of your technology gadgets, like your phones and tablets. I know this can prove difficult for some, but you need to have fewer distractions. Facebook CEO Sheryl Sandberg says switching off her phones at night is an excellent way to rest and avoid distractions.

- Make efforts to relax appropriately before bedtime so you can sleep with ease. For example, avoid eating heavy meals for one or two hours before bedtime.

- It helps if you have the right ambiance and lighting to sleep well at night. Therefore, avoid too much light in your room by switching off the bright lights. If you must leave the light on, then go for colored or warm lights.

- If you are new to waking up early, please take it slowly. Try waking up 15-30 minutes earlier than your usual time. After three days, you can increase your wake up time to between 45 minutes and one hour to achieve the 5 A.M. goal. This strategy will help reduce the strain on your body at first.

- Strive to maintain a routine with exercises. Instead of heavy sessions of one hour or more per day, make them light exercise sessions of maybe 30 minutes daily. The goal is not to wear you out or make it burdensome, but exciting.

- Take the liberty to wear whatever clothing your organization's culture permits, but always look for the best ways to combine colors and clothing to simplify your life.

- If your work schedule starts much later, the 8 A.M. club might be more appropriate for you instead of the 5 A.M. Club. Stick to what helps you increase personal productivity using Sharma's 20/20/20 formula.

Joining the 5 A.M. club gives you the time to take charge of your day. You have ample time to ruminate on issues and use the power of imagination to design or visualize your day. You can spend more time learning or doing research on the things you need to actualize your goals. That will help boost your energy to accomplish much.

Chapter Summary

This chapter looked at how your morning hours can affect personal productivity. Robin Sharma's 5 A.M. Club was used as a prototype to help you increase your performance. Take-homes from this chapter include:

- Highly successful people possess work habits that help them excel.

- Robin Sharma's 5 A.M. club breaks down what you should do during the first hour of waking up.

- Work out your days with Sharma's 20/20/20 formula.

- Exercise for the first twenty minutes, plan your day with another twenty minutes and study for the last twenty minutes.

- The study time allows you to learn a new skill or improve your skills in your career path.

- Studying for at least twenty minutes every day will help boost personal productivity.

- To excel at the 5 A.M. club, you need to balance your sleeping and waking times. Do not deny yourself adequate sleep because you need sufficient sleep to meet your goals. Instead, adjust your sleeping time to cover any shortfall in sleep time.

- Waking up quite early to start your day increases your mental alertness.

- The 5 A.M. club teaches you how to incorporate discipline into your day, which is something highly successful people do.

- Meditation is an integral part of your life and work schedule as it helps fine-tune your life, setting it up for progress.

In the next chapter, we shall be looking at how to create a personal Kanban to help you prioritize and organize tasks efficiently.

CHAPTER THREE

CREATE YOUR PERSONAL KANBAN TO PRIORITIZE AND ORGANIZE TASKS

Life can sometimes become more complicated than you desire. Attending to customers, going through the motions of a 9 to 5 job, coping with the enormous bills at home, and more, all tend to make life hectic. We try to find answers about how to organize our priorities or how many tasks we can handle each day or week. We struggle with what tasks to take care of first and what other tasks to delegate.

Whether it is a small, medium, or large scale organization, prioritizing will always remain a veritable tool for success. Achieving personal productivity at work, academics, or with personal relationships requires the ability to organize tasks effectively. That's precisely why you need to understand how to create a personal Kanban for personal and workplace goals.

What Is Personal Kanban About?

The Personal Kanban is a model developed by Jim Benson and Tonianne DeMaria Barry. Kanban is a commonly used software by Agile IT experts to prioritize important tasks and engaging tasks, as well as to maximize time. It is an abridged and easy-to-use version of the Kanban methods designed to help improve your productivity. Personal Kanban allows individuals, either professionals or students, to become more efficient. Jim Benson's idea of personal Kanban is to simplify your life and take away the hassles of everyday living. Trying to take on too much can prove disastrous, and there is only so much an individual can handle alone. Hence, a lot of tasks get done shabbily or are left hanging for too long.

Jim and Tonianne's Kanban approach shows you how to prioritize your tasks by entering them into the system as *backlog* or *ready*. It makes it easier to determine the tasks that are actually of higher priority. With personal Kanban, you can track your work progress at the end of each week. You can identify the completed tasks and pending ones.

The personal Kanban involves a simple visualization of all of your responsibilities utilizing a whiteboard (or post-it notes) to indicate progression. To excel at prioritizing, you can create a structure for your tasks, creating three columns on the whiteboard. Each column will cover a specific category of tasks: *backlog* (which is ready), *doing*, and *done*.

To take control of your life, the personal Kanban is a powerful tool. Moreover, it works for every type of responsibility and goal-setting need to enhance workflow.

Why You Should Prioritize Tasks

Prioritization has to do with deciding on what activity is the most important to your goal so that you can attend to it first. It's the process of arranging tasks based on their order of relevance to your day-to-day goals or objectives.

More Value for Your Time

Time is a limited resource made available to everyone equally as 24 hours a day, 7 days a week, and 365 days in a year. Sometimes people spend their time on less valuable things. Not that those things are not essential, but they might not add as much value to your bottom line.

To increase your productivity, you need to spend more time doing things that are not only important, but also not as urgent. Learning to prioritize your time using the Kanban model will help you to get more value for the time you spend working.

Better Organized and Focused

Instead of doing things haphazardly, do a few things at a time, but in a better way. Personal Kanban teaches us to do the right work at the appropriate time. With a to-do list or a well-laid-out Kanban plan, you can organize your personal and work goals. It will help you to break down your weekly and monthly goals into smaller daily tasks.

Once you can achieve this structure, you become more focused on achieving your goals.

Increases Productivity and Profitability

With your personal Kanban, you should experience an improvement in your productivity. Increased productivity will result in a higher profit. Spending quality time on the things that produce a higher result in your career naturally leads to more profit and success.

Basic Principles of the Personal Kanban

The personal Kanban thrives on two basic principles, which are:

- Visualizing your work.

- Limiting your work progress.

Visualize Your Work

Visualizing your work is an excellent way to move concepts or other hectic, work-related activity into simple actions. Research has shown that the human brain responds faster and better to images or visuals than to words by at least 90%. Also, the human mind can process images 60,000 times faster than it can process text. Therefore, the Kanban works intrinsically as a visual task planning platform. It helps you visualize your tasks and simplify the task implementation process.

Limiting Your Work Progress

As a human, we sometimes try to act like superhumans with the ability to do more than we are capable of. We take on several tasks at the same time and end up with shoddy quality work. Recent research confirms that the human brain cannot carry out multiple tasks successfully at optimal levels. Hence, you will discover that some tasks get done better while others turn out badly.

When you limit your work progress, it doesn't mean denying yourself the opportunity to do more. Limiting your work progress makes it easier to focus on specific tasks and see them through to completion. Limited work progress makes it necessary to take on responsibilities that you can finish over time and stick through to the end. It takes away the problem of having several unfinished projects, breeding frustration.

Limiting work progress helps you give more value to your time in prioritizing each task before you. You learn to prioritize tasks and identify the most critical job to deal with each time.

The Personal Kanban mantra encourages you to start and finish a task before proceeding to the next. Your productivity will improve when not running several projects at the same time (multitasking).

It helps if you don't have to handle every job. Other strategies to get more done include delegation or outsourcing of tasks, instead of trying to do everything yourself. When you first get on the personal Kanban plan, your initial reaction will be a feeling of awkwardness. Most times, it feels like your life is under external control. If you are a person who gets personal satisfaction from juggling several activities, it will at first feel like you are under-performing. The impression that you are getting less work done is not accurate. Once you allow yourself to live within the WIP Limits (Work-In-Process), you will discover you have achieved far more over time. The results will be of exceptional quality and better for your corporate and personal goals. Even your clients and family will notice the improvement.

Negative Effects of Multitasking

I have been a victim of trying to multitask on several separate activities before. When I began my consulting career, I tried juggling the preparation of a business plan development task, seminar paper, and coordinating a social event. All the while I was making calls, sending emails, and trying to gather more facts for my business plan. I also had to make calls to caterers, media teams, event decorators, and more, so the event could go smoothly. Well, It all ended in a fiasco as I left out some vital aspects of the event. Only last-minute face-saving measures saved the day. As for my business plan, it wasn't ready for pitching at the appropriate time. And that's the reason you need to limit your work progress using the personal Kanban board. Some of the adverse effects of multitasking include:

Lowers Your IQ

Research conducted by the University of London shows that multitasking tends to lower your IQ by at least 17%. The effect of multitasking is similar to a person who has smoked marijuana or had a sleepless night. The individual ends up storing fewer details from the multitasked sessions.

Reduces Brain Efficiency

The American Psychological Association published an article in the Journal of Experimental Psychology on multitasking. It indicated that multitasking reduces the brain's ability to process issues faster. To process multiple tasks means shifting the brain's gear from one item to another, and that takes time. The brain has to make the shift by turning off one cognitive rule for another goal.

What's more, research at the University of Sussex states that multitasking can impair the brain.

How to Use the Personal Kanban Board

The personal Kanban board is comprised of 3 distinct columns that help you prioritize your tasks. The three columns contain the 'To Do,' 'Doing,' and 'Done' sections. The 'To Do' section is also known as the 'Option.'

Column 1: To-Do or Option

Under column one, write down every goal or task you have in mind to do. There are two strategies to adopt here. Write down 3-5 of your most critical tasks in the column. The second strategy involves writing down all of the assignments you intend on carrying out, no matter how many. When it's time to implement, you then decide the tasks to advance to the next column.

Things to include in column one can consist of work and personal goals. Workplace tasks include meeting with suppliers by Monday at 10 A.M., submitting a proposal to a specific client by noon, paying for insurance, drafting letters to prospective clients, replying to emails and inquiry, etc.. For personal tasks, you could include seeing your physician by Wednesday at 2 P.M., taking your puppy out for a walk every evening, attending your kids' valedictorian ceremony on Friday by 10 A.M., etc..

With this in mind, you can create a custom plan for your 'To Do' column to cover workplace tasks and personal tasks. Personal responsibilities can include spiritual, financial, health, education, or social goals. When selecting a job to complete, focus on those that take you faster toward your long-term goals. Following the personal Kanban board will make you focus on the most important tasks instead of the most urgent ones for completion.

Column 2: Doing or In Progress

Each task should already have a timeline for execution. Once it is time to execute a particular job, you transfer that task from the 'To Do' to the 'In Progress' column. For instance, once you want to accomplish any item under your personal goal, such as seeing your doctor, you move it to 'In Progress' under column two. However, avoid adding too many items into the 'In Progress' column to avoid over-burdening yourself. If you somehow feel you have more than you can handle, please feel free to move some items back to the 'To Do' column once again. It is better to finish a smaller amount of tasks under column two before transferring more from column one.

Before this, however, you need to set up a WIP (Work-In-Progress) Limit. The WIP Limit refers to the maximum or allowed amount of tasks you should handle per time. These tasks should go to the 'In Progress' column two. Thus, you deliberately force yourself to focus all of your energy on accomplishing only those tasks.

And in most cases, those tasks make up what you can achieve with success. Remember, create standard WIP Limits and always stick to it.

Column 3: Done

Only a completed task should be included in the 'Doing' or 'Done' column. However, some jobs require a follow-up or can come up again in your list of tasks. At that point, you can re-introduce a task into column one before the 'Doing' list. That means, if you have seen your doctor this week, it should move to the 'Done' column, but if you have another appointment to see your doctor on a new date, then it can come under the 'To Do' column one again.

Every time a task successfully translates from column one, 'To Do' to column three, 'Done,' it evokes a feeling of fulfillment. That feeling helps to inspire you to get more tasks done. Following this process on the Kanban board will make the picture clearer and more exciting. Over time, you will discover an increase in your productivity level. The passion for getting more done will become stronger.

Creating Your Personal Kanban Board

You can create your personal Kanban board with ease. All you require is a whiteboard and Post-Its or stickies to begin making your board. Also, you can create a Microsoft Excel sheet or Word document containing the required columns and rows. Create a note with your preferred option with the three columns: 'To Do,' 'In Progress' (Doing), and 'Done.'

Besides using a whiteboard, you can make use of online task management tools like the free Trello tool or Asana. These tools allow you to create tasks and prioritize them.

Guidelines for Using the Personal Kanban

- Avoid overcrowding column one, 'To Do.' However, if it becomes necessary and due to the volume of tasks at hand, then include the tasks, by all means.

- Create a specific timeline for achieving each of these tasks so that you know when to move them to column two.

- Ensure that you do a scale of preference by placing the most critical job at the top of your 'To Do' column.

- It is also possible to have a separate column between columns one and two. Call this column 'Prioritized Tasks,' or column 1A. If you have too many tasks in column one, move the high-value tasks to 'Prioritized Tasks,' leaving the others for the general-purpose tasks. You can intermittently move tasks into column 1A before they get to the 'In Progress' stage.

- Regularly review and update your Kanban board. In line with your goal, the Kanban board should be reviewed daily or weekly to identify disparity or to update activities.

- If the tasks become more than your new schedule can cope with, then learn to outsource or delegate some tasks.

Simple Tips for Prioritizing Tasks

- Write down all of your tasks in a single location (the personal Kanban).

- Organize or prioritize your tasks using the personal Kanban. To effectively prioritize your tasks before writing them on the Personal Kanban, you can categorize them into the following:

- Do — Tasks that require urgent attention.

- Defer — Task that should be done later.

- Delegate — Tasks that you need others to handle or outsource.

- Delete — Tasks that might not offer much value or have stayed too long on the list.

The Eisenhower Matrix can help you to determine what should be in your To-Do list.

- Choose between planning the task for each day the evening before or early in the morning. If you revise the assignments for each day in the evening, then it will be easier to plan for the next day's tasks too.

- Be proactive about how you handle each day's job. Take the driver's seat by not reacting to activities, but by determining how each day's task should proceed.

- Create spare time for family, friends, and other non-work related activities. Relaxing and socializing can put you in a better frame of mind to get more tasks done productively.

- Be as flexible as things might need to be. Assignments that are not completed can be placed in the personal Kanban for another day.

- Pay more attention to those tasks that will have more effect on your long-term goals. Focus on the tasks that give you more results and not just the ones that are keeping you busy.

- You can have an accountability partner, someone who will hold you to your goals.

Chapter Summary

This chapter focused extensively on the following:

- Trying to cope with each day's activities can take its toll on your productivity, which is why you need to understand how to prioritize your life.

- Your personal and career goals can create a source of conflict; therefore, the personal Kanban can help prioritize your tasks better.

- The Personal Kanban is a productivity or task management system that allows individuals to prioritize each task for accomplishment.

- Prioritizing tasks helps you get more value out of limited time to make you more productive.

- The two basic principles of the Personal Kanban include visualizing your work and limiting your work progress.

- Visualizing your work involves creating a mental block by which your key performance can improve.

- Research shows that images have a 93% greater chance of making an impression on the human mind than text.

- Limiting your work progress is an attempt to say 'no' to taking on more tasks than you can on average complete in a day or week.

- WIP Limit refers to setting a specific number of tasks to accomplish without overburdening yourself or hindering your productivity level.

- Multitasking can result in less productivity.

- To use the Personal Kanban, you need to create three columns containing 'To Do,' 'In Progress' (or Doing), and 'Done.'

- The To-Do column should contain 3-5 (or more) tasks you need to accomplish in line with your goals.

- The In Progress or Doing column should list the jobs you are now ready to execute.

- The Done column should contain all of the completed assignments.

- It is best if you prioritize your tasks beginning with the most important, rather than the most urgent.

- Move each task from column one to the other as you make progress.

- The Personal Kanban should be made simple and not complicated.

- It helps if you have a whiteboard and Post-Its to create your Personal Kanban.

- Review the Personal Kanban regularly to update and improve it.

In the next chapter, you will learn the dangers of procrastination and how to overcome it.

CHAPTER FOUR

HOW TO OVERCOME PROCRASTINATION

Procrastination is a thief of time, like Edward Young rightly called it. In terms of productivity, procrastination is one major factor that hinders people from taking giant strides in life. It prevents people from making the right decisions at the right times or taking prompt actions toward achieving specific goals. In many ways, procrastination has kept a whole lot of individuals in the trap of working harder rather than smarter.

Opportunities tend to slip off the fingers when the time that should have gone into productive use slowly slips away.

Procrastination does not necessarily mean laziness, but a delay in carrying out a course. Based on research, Piers Steel states that nearly 95% of humans procrastinate to varying degrees. Many find themselves slaves to this habitual attitude and wish they could overcome procrastination. Even personal dreams and efforts end up a victim of procrastination. People run this cycle for years without any meaningful action toward one's desired goals.

Procrastination can hurt productivity. It often results in low self-esteem, depression, frustration, inadequacies, and guilt. Rather than beating yourself up, deliberate and concrete steps toward overcoming this trait should be the focal point. The fight against procrastination requires action. A procrastinator who wants to make headway in life must understand that the time to start is now. Overcoming procrastination is possible, but is a gradual process only achievable if you are willing to take the necessary steps.

The following steps will help you to overcome the scourge of procrastination:

Step 1: Admit It, You Do Procrastinate

The first step toward any self-actualizing pursuit is to identify that you have a problem that needs urgent attention or assistance. Telling yourself the truth makes the journey a rather short one. Putting off things indefinitely or getting distracted on a focal activity is not a healthy lifestyle for the highly successful. Here are some ways to check if procrastination has become your lifestyle:

Leaving Important Tasks Undone

Many people still fall victim to leaving the important stuff undone due to distraction and the inability to prioritize. People sometimes start a task with a lot of enthusiasm and then, due to pressure, distraction, challenges, and more, they abandon these tasks halfway. When something else comes up, they jump on that and forget what they were working on. If this act becomes habitual, then procrastination will become a lifestyle.

Abandoning High Priority Tasks for Something Less Critical

Some schools of thought believe dealing with the smaller tasks will give you the motivation to take on bigger assignments. Another school of thought believes the best part of your day should go to dealing with the most challenging tasks. However, some people take on smaller tasks but later push the bigger ones to oblivion. The danger here is that the high priority tasks end up not getting any attention.

Besides, pursuing the less critical tasks while precious time slips away can be counter-productive. And once you get accustomed to responding to urgent and pressing issues first, instead of learning how to deal with essential tasks, it becomes a habit that is hard to break.

Using Your Time for Others to Your Detriment

It's good to help and to try to solve work-related issues for others. However, allowing others to determine how your day goes is a recipe for failure.

Getting caught in the web of doing tasks for friends and family first could be a real time-waster out of your limited work hours. While it is not a bad thing to assist family, friends, and colleagues, it should not be to the detriment of your own work. Let all assistance go into your To-Do list so that it can fit into your program, rather than superseding your other tasks.

Waiting for the Right Time, Mood, or Condition

It is an illusion to assume that there is the right time, mood, or condition to get anything meaningful done. And too many people have become a victim of their own emotions and timing. Waiting for the right condition, or the 'perfect' time that never seems to come has plunged many into wasted years of not achieving anything tangible. Your mood could create an excuse for procrastination, stating the time is not right, or that all of the factors are not in place for smooth execution.

However, the truth is, there will never be a perfect time or the right mood to get anything done. Also, the conditions for accomplishing your goals might not always align. For this reason, you are in the best position to dictate to yourself what the right mood, time, and condition should be. As long as you want to, all excuses will give way to you.

"He that is good for making excuses is seldom good for anything else."– Benjamin Franklin.

"The trouble with excuses in that they become inevitably difficult to believe after they've been used a couple of times."– Scott Spencer

Spending More Time on Less Important Activities

All tasks deserve your attention, but not all jobs require equal attention. Therefore, the ability to know the amount of time to devote to each task will determine your level of productivity. This is the formula used by top performers to excel. Reading and replying to emails is an important task but might not require as much time as developing your seminar paper. For customer support staff, reading and responding to emails could carry more importance than writing the daily report during critical work hours. That means, for each person, specific tasks carry more significance than others. The ability to spend time appropriately on the right jobs will determine the extent of your productivity.

You No Longer Trust Yourself

When people get into the habit of breaking promises to themselves, trust becomes impossible. When there is a lack of confidence in one's ability, their productivity will begin to dwindle. It becomes impossible to find the motivation to do anything since they believe the tasks are not likely to see fruition, and so they give up.

Giving Up Easily

Giving up at the slightest challenge can become a good excuse to procrastinate. Once people face situations that look insurmountable, the tendency to quit becomes higher. Many times, the thought of going back becomes a great struggle. With too much time gone by, an overwhelming feeling begins to set in, leading to more procrastination.

Step 2: Find Out Why You Procrastinate and Deal With It

Everyone has what it takes to excel in implementing tasks, but most people lack the discipline and knowledge to make things work. The irony is that most people do not admit to themselves that one of their most significant problems is procrastination. Some of those who do know cannot explain the reason they procrastinate or lack the discipline to overcome it.

Writing yourself off is not the way to go; you have to work it out. However, you first need to identify the real cause of your procrastination. Here are some factors responsible for procrastination:

Lack of Interest

Once a person is not passionate about what they do, the tendency to procrastinate becomes higher. Delays or complete avoidance become the order of the day when you feel low about what you do. The only way out of such a logjam is to find your sparks.

For managers, assigning a task to somebody should follow specific criteria in order to succeed. Looking at a person's perspective on a task could go a long way in determining if they are the right person for the task. Here is what to do:

Decide On the Most Suitable Person for the Job

Delegating the responsibility to a person who is more likely to get it done is critical. Some people have a high tolerance level for particular tasks and assigning it to such people will result in bigger gains.

Break the Work Into Bits of Tasks

If one's tolerance level is low, breaking the job into smaller components will help. Try to concentrate on smaller chunks per time.

Schedule Time

Designating a particular time to get the task started is a good idea. Once you commence the duties, focus on completing those tasks before picking up another. Doing this will increase productivity and reduce having too many uncompleted tasks.

Lack of Motivation

The best way to go about the motivation factor is actually to start the task. Waiting for the right motivation might take a while and delay the job longer than is necessary. Once a project begins and you start seeing some level of success, the motivation level tends to increase. We will talk more about motivation in chapter eight.

Dealing with Personal Issues

Personal challenges can stand in the way of getting things done. When life's other challenges arise, the ability to handle them properly will determine whether or not it will harm your work. Therefore, the ability to manage your emotions in the face of challenges will determine the quality of work done.

However, in challenging situations, it is best to create a priority for managing tasks, as well as to break them into smaller chunks that you can handle. Focusing so much on your challenges will only result in a drop in productivity, but trying to look ahead will give you the energy to keep working.

Deficiency in Skills

People let their goals slide due to their tolerance level, focus, energy levels, or a lack of one skill or the other. Because of this, you must develop skills in the areas that will help you to advance your goals. Mentoring also provides an avenue to learn from those who have excelled in the same field as yours. Reading is another means to develop yourself or to learn from others within your area. The point is, if you must overcome the issue of procrastination, all activities that trigger procrastination need to go—and one way to fight procrastination is self-development.

Taking a look at the bigger picture, if procrastination is stealing your time, what will you do to stop it? Self-development can serve as a fortification against procrastination.

Fear

Fear is oppositional to faith and courage. People sometimes leave essential tasks undone due to the fear of the volume of the tasks. Unfortunately, delaying the job will only complicate issues as you run out of time.

There are too many fears in people's lives. There is the fear of failure, of the unknown, of negative feedback, and of rejection. For many, the fear of being evaluated or getting negative feedback denies them the zest to even start. Feedback is an integral part of measuring how productive you are and should not create a source of fear. See feedback as a tool to improve your productivity.

Whatever the form of fear is, this has hindered many from taking bold steps into starting new projects, moving to the next level in their personal and career life.

Feeling Anxious or Overwhelmed

Anxiety is a major cause of procrastination. Once a person is worried about certain things, they tend to procrastinate, and as the task delays, it leads to further anxiety over the non-completion of the task, while the cause of the tension remains.

As the events become more ugly, and task after task begins piling up, there is a tendency for you to feel overwhelmed. If you do not take prompt action to resolve the issues, seek assistance with the tasks, or complete tasks, depression can set in. Anxiety can create a crippling effect or mindset. However, with concerted effort, you can get things back on track.

Perceived Lack of Control

When people feel they are not in control of the circumstances of their lives, the tendency to procrastinate increases. Such people view external influences, such as the environment or other people, as being in control of their circumstances. Feeling helpless can cause depression or a feeling of worthlessness and cause the victim to delay tasks.

A sense of not being appreciated by a critical boss or parent can make one feel helpless. This feeling can slow down work progress or result in low quality work.

Step 3: Toughen-Up Against Procrastination: Strategies to Help

To overcome procrastination as a habit takes a conscious and deliberate effort. Research shows that it takes around 66 days to develop a new habit or to drop an existing one. Therefore, to achieve this goal, you must be able to unlearn and relearn. Unlearn the old way of doing things and relearn the new way to get things done. Changing habits doesn't happen overnight but requires a process involving persistence and patience.

How to Overcome Procrastination

You can overcome procrastination using the following strategies over time:

Learn to Forgive Past Procrastination

Don't be too harsh on yourself; let go of past procrastination. The inability to complete a specific task in the past or the non-attainment of a goal can be a severe mind stump. More often than not, people tend to allow past failures to stand in the way when trying to move ahead. However, holding onto the past will only increase the chance of a recurrence. If you must excel, then you have to find a way to let go of past failures.

The first thing to do is to realize it is just a weakness. As long as it is a habit, you can unlearn the same way you developed the habit of procrastinating.

Establish Your Goals

Get clearly defined goals and SMART goals in line with your personal and career objectives. Setting unrealistic goals can lead to further frustration, making your fight against procrastination difficult. To make your goals achievable, remember to write them down, as well as to set timelines for achieving them. There are several tools in this book to help you with setting realistic goals and seeing them come to pass, so keep reading to know more.

Commit to the Task

As stated earlier in this book, taking action is as necessary as setting goals. If you set goals and will not commit the needed time and resources to actualize them, then they will amount to nothing. You must make a concerted effort to develop skills, find out what you need, draw up a plan of action, and pursue the goals vigorously.

Focus On the End

Having a mindset of completion can help motivate you toward attaining your goals. You can focus on the outcome by visualizing what you want to achieve through that goal. But to succeed, you must have already drawn up a plan of action to achieve that goal. In this way, focusing on the end helps you to visualize achieving the goal.

In addition, focusing on a task will not remove the challenges that go with every job, but having a plan of action and a well-written goal will help keep you motivated and adjust your strategy as the need arises. To help you focus better, all distractions have to be dealt with to succeed.

Celebrate Small Successes

Promise yourself a reward for the completion of every milestone and give it to yourself. After all, you deserve it! It could be a treat to your favorite eatery at lunchtime. The excitement will boost your spirit when small successes are visible. If you do not celebrate yourself, who will?

Be Responsible for Someone

Asking someone to check up on you and your activities can be helpful. Knowing that you are answerable to someone else will boost your morale to complete tasks. Where a personal buddy is not readily available, applications like remote bliss can be a valuable tool.

Peer pressure provides an effective support system. Once friends and family are in the know about your goals, they are bound to keep asking about the progress.

Act On the Go

As soon as you receive new projects, place a priority on them by not allowing them to linger for so long without assigning them. By that, I mean work them into your To-Do list with a timeline and a plan of action. When you do that with each new task, you will feel more confident and in charge of your day as nothing gets past you. As a technique to avoid procrastination, never leave any tasks unattended.

Identify your most and least productive time, and schedule high and low priority tasks to fit these timings. Knowing when you are most productive will help you focus on the more important tasks on your To-Do list. Completing critical goals makes working on others less difficult or frustrating.

Rephrase Your Internal Thought Processes

What you say to yourself, over time, becomes what you believe. The phrases you use will either inspire or put a clog on the wheels of progress. Phrases like 'have to' or 'need to' suggest that one has no choice at all. Such comments alone can demotivate. Whereas phrases like 'I must' and 'I choose to' are pointers to the fact that you are in control.

Eliminate Distractions

Distractions are the greatest enemy to achieving your goals, and they can come in different forms: television, emails, social media, phone calls, as well as family and friends. Distractions can consume your most productive time, leaving you with unaccomplished dreams.

A good plan at minimizing or eliminating distractions will leave you with more time to concentrate on the task at hand. Even if the need arises, you can place your phone on mute and stay off technology tools that can distract you from your job.

Focus On Less Pleasant Tasks First

Deal with any tasks that can drain your energy first, while your energy levels are still high. Leaving energy-draining tasks until later might result in their being left undone. Other less draining jobs will not be so challenging to handle.

Change Your Environment

It might become necessary to have a different environment from the one you are already used to. Environments have a way of impacting your productivity. They can be a source of inspiration or a reason to procrastinate.

Certain conditions make a work environment unpleasant or productive, and they include:

- Hostility

- Poorly-arranged workstations

- Prejudice

- Shortage of work tools and supplies

- Faulty equipment

- Stuffy, damp, hot or cold environments

Procrastination can become second nature or habit. It takes a concerted effort, strong will, dedication, and a plan of action to deal with it. Overcoming your problem of procrastination will come with time, not overnight.

Action is key. Once you understand why you procrastinate and your areas of weakness, then you are on your way to dealing with them. Now, the time has come, will you delay (procrastinate) putting these plans to work?

Chapter Summary

- First, accept that you procrastinate and take concrete steps to overcome it.

- Get an understanding of the things people do that has made procrastination a lifestyle.

- From the list, identify why you are procrastinating and get to work immediately.

- Realize that procrastination is a shortcoming a lot of people have and forgive yourself.

- Choose the best anti-procrastination strategies that best suit you. Be sure they will work for you.

- Having a motivating mindset, focus on the end of the task rather than on the beginning.

- Don't work alone. Make yourself accountable to someone for checks and balances.

- Act as you go. Commit to the task and avoid a build-up that will encourage a relapse into procrastination. Just get into the action plan.

- As much as possible, keep distracting factors away from you. Develop a will not to indulge in them.

- Celebrate every successful milestone with a reward. A personal pat on the back can be highly motivating.

- By all means, change environments if need be. They have a way of putting you in high spirits for maximum output.

- What you perceive is what you believe. Mind the words you say to yourself. Change your internal dialogue to suit your new resolve.

In the next chapter, you will learn about the value of maximizing time and time management hacks.

CHAPTER FIVE

HACKS TO MAXIMIZE YOUR TIME MANAGEMENT

Time is a limited, but universal resource, and everyone has an equal share of 24 hours daily to accomplish much. However, not everyone makes the best use of their time. If not, how do you explain the fact that some people attain a higher degree of success than some others within the same 24 hour time frame? Does it mean highly successful people spend longer hours working than the less successful? The answer is: no! The simple fact is that some people have learned the art of managing their time more effectively. Others, however, might have more issues with time-wasters in their schedule. Therefore, how do you manage time to increase your productivity?

"Time isn't the main thing; it is the only thing."- Miles Davis

Explosive Time Management Tips for Increased Productivity

Here are time-tested, yet simple time management hacks to help you get on the road to greater efficiency:

Audit Time Spent

When you do a time audit, it will amaze you to discover where the bulk of your time goes. How much time do you spend on work and non-work related activities? How much time do you spend on tasks that will improve your bottom line and push you closer to your goals? How much time goes into checking and responding to emails, social media, and more? You might intend on spending only 30 minutes on emails and social media every morning, but end up spending over an hour.

Start by tracking your activities for a whole week to see areas of time wastage. One of the simplest ways to track your operations is by using time tracking applications like Toggl, RescueTime, or Calendar. At the end of the week, the app report will give you a better idea of how your time flies. Now, you can be in a better position to make the needed adjustments.

Time Each Task and Set Limits

Keeping the deadlines open is a recipe for getting nothing done on time or at all. Setting a timeline or restrictions for each task keeps you from procrastinating or delaying them. Creating buffers around your tasks makes it easier to manage a particular job. For a task that requires several days or weeks to accomplish, breaking them into smaller, manageable daily tasks can help. Each milestone achieved brings you closer to your overall goal.

I use buffers in helping to accomplish a task. When I have a speaking engagement, I like planning weeks ahead. Therefore, I usually create a timeline with buffers to help me complete the seminar paper on schedule. If, for any reason, the paper takes a longer time than scheduled, then it has to wait for another time slot. That's the only way to avoid eating into time for other activities.

However, make sure the timelines are not bogus, but something you can achieve in reality. You can get someone to hold you accountable by letting them know what you want to achieve and the timeframe assigned to achieve it. Your accountability buddy can help ensure you stay on track for success.

"It takes as much energy to wish as it takes to plan."- Eleanor Roosevelt

Plan Ahead

"Measure twice, cut once" is a popular proverb in the building construction or carpentry world. It focuses on engineers or carpenters getting things right on the first attempt. And that's how valuable planning ahead is to your goals.

Having a plan of action will save you the stress of wandering or focusing on the less critical tasks. Some tasks are more vital to your success than others. Without adequate planning, you can end up achieving very little.

Best Time to Create a Plan or To-Do List:

Start the Night Before

At the end of each day's work can be the perfect time to make plans for the next day's activities. As little as 15-30 minutes is what you need to create a To-Do list of the most important assignments for tomorrow.

The exciting thing about planning ahead the evening before is that it helps you eliminate likely distractions. Doing your plan ahead of tomorrow puts your mind in top gear and readiness for tomorrow's activities. This can also help to motivate you and get you excited about work. It also increases your focus and channels your energy toward your most productive tasks for the day.

Start First Thing In the Morning

While some people prefer planning their day the night before, others do so first thing in the morning. You can make a list of 3 or 5 of your most urgent and important activities for the day. Then, set a timeline on your most productive time to achieve them.

However, always do a review or double-check your plans to avoid errors or mistakes. Any mix up with your schedule or activities can result in wasting more time trying to remedy the situation.

Say No to Multitasking

Multitasking or task hopping is a productivity killer. The erroneous belief that juggling several tasks at the same time will help you get more done is not true. Research confirms that carrying on several tasks at a time can have a negative toll on the human brain. Multitasking can also result in lower quality work. More so, you end up spending a longer time multitasking as your mind tries to make the shift between two tasks.

For this reason, the solution is single-tasking. Make it a habit to start and finish tasks before moving on to the other. You can set timelines, milestones, and timers to put you on the right track, one task at a time. Intentionally develop your mindset to focus on one task.

Protect Your 'In the Zone' Time

What time of the day are you most productive? The best time to schedule a demanding task is at the time you are more alert mentally. You can schedule that time into your calendar or To-Do list.

Protecting your 'in the zone' time is the same as understanding your patterns. We all have habits, but the idea is to pick up healthy habits that help increase personal productivity. Each person has a time of the day they are most productive. The best time to get certain tasks done should be at the time you get your burst of energy. For instance, if you think best in the morning, after working out, after lunchtime, or late at night, then create a schedule around that time. However, it will depend on the type of goal you wish to achieve: personal or workplace.

Science proposes four hours of work a day as all you need. Sounds absurd? Well, it doesn't necessarily mean you only get to execute tasks for four hours and play for twenty hours. It says to focus on the most critical tasks using your most productive hours of four hours in a day. The rest of the hours could go to resolving less demanding tasks.

Keep Meetings on Task

Staff meetings constitute an integral part of strategic planning, re-appraisal, and continuous work assessment. However, to make staff meetings fruitful and productive, they must be streamlined and follow laid down procedures. Allowing a meeting to run without a To-Do list or Agenda might end without concrete decisions being reached. You must provide clear directions for any meeting and set timelines and objectives for each item on the list.

Each meeting must start and end on time. Also, some organizations make it a habit to call meetings too often. You can resolve some issues without meeting with everyone. With the aid of technology, some tools make it easier to disseminate information and get feedback without calling frequent meetings. Tools like Trello, Zoom, Slack, and Asana allow groups to discuss and share ideas without stretching work time. Another strategy could involve scheduling regular weekly or monthly meetings and reports, instead of impromptu meetings.

Create Email Handling Time

Emails can be a major source of distraction, and you must be deliberate about how to handle your messages. As much as important messages can come in, you do not want emails directing how your work flows daily. The problem with responding to emails as they come in is that you become more reactive than in charge of your day. The solution is to have a time scheduled for reading and responding to emails.

To help concentrate on the most productive tasks, I usually have specific times for responding to emails. Usually, two to three times a day is ideal for email handling, but never around your productive time.

One strategy I use is to select the email messages to open, read, and respond to at specific times. When responding, make sure the responses do not exceed five sentences to save time.

Turn Off Notifications

Notifications are quite helpful in keeping you up to date with email and social media messages. They can, however, also serve as a major source of distraction and make you lose focus on important tasks. Important notifications can come from your email or social media feeds, but to manage them properly, only enable those notifications that will help you advance your tasks and goals. Even at that, it still may not be necessary to enable notifications on your PC and all of your smart devices. Such acts only increase the chances for distraction.

Alternatively, you can disable notifications when working on your most demanding tasks. When you complete the tasks, push notification can be enabled again.

Watch Your Social Media Usage

Facebook, Twitter, Instagram, SnapCatch, and more is an interesting sport that serves different purposes for people. However, staying on social media for too long can be distracting. Therefore, you need to limit the amount of time spent there deliberately. However, some businesses use it as part of their business tool. If you are a social media manager, run ads, have an eCommerce store, or monitor customer support, create a concrete plan for social media usage.

Whatever your social media needs, have a to-do plan that incorporates it and creates timelines for it. Arrange its usage in a way that allows you to do more productive activities. If it is more of a social tool, then keep it social and civil.

Buffer Up! Cut Yourself Some Slack

Cut yourself some slack by incorporating buffer times into your schedule. You are a human, and your brain needs time to cool off. The human brain, by default, is not a twenty hour fully operational machine. Certain mental and physical functions of the brain need rest so that they can maintain peak performance. Hence, research shows that the brain works critically on average 90-minute per time before a decline. After this time, your brain needs some form of distraction to remain motivated and focused.

It's not a sign of diligence or hard work to remain on your desk all day. Fortunately, other non-critical tasks or activities do crop up in the course of your day, and that may be the best time to attend to them. However, moving from one mentally demanding task or meeting to another isn't a brilliant idea or a productive way to live either. Rather, help your body refuel by meditating, taking a walk, or simply daydreaming. It will help clear your mind.

Besides work, having a buffer time can give you ample time to get to the next meeting early. Your schedule should have such buffers as much as it allows you to get through one activity to the other. It should also allow you time to unwind and rejuvenate. Schedule your activities like this: a big chunk of a task, with bite-sized buffers. About 25 to 30 minutes of buffer-time should be ideal.

Be Fair to Yourself

You are the most vital aspect of your work schedule or task. Without you, there would be no task accomplished; therefore, take good care of yourself. If you fall ill, burn out, or lose your life, someone else will take your place. Yes, your legacy will live on, but your family and friends will have to face the pain of your sudden departure. Even if you do not lose your life, developing health complications will only slow down your productivity and make it impossible for you to pursue your lofty ideas and goals.

Take out time to relax, have fun, exercise regularly, eat healthily, and to spend time with family and friends. Sometimes, it pays to do what pleases you. Be selfish! Take a vacation. In the end, use the motivation and experience to get your brilliant ideas or tasks done.

I have a spacious office with a work table, a small conference room, and a living room. When I go through demanding tasks, sometimes I unwind for a few minutes by relocating to the living room. I can lay on the sofa, allow some distraction by seeing a program on television, listen to music, or a sitcom. I do anything other than work. And when I'm back at my desk, I'm all fired up, ready to go!

Use the 80/20 Rule or Pareto Principle

The 80/20 law states that 80% of your results or successes come from 20% of the effort put into them. So, does that mean you only need to spend 20% of your time working? Or, should you come into work just one day a week, after all, that's 20%. No!

The Pareto principle means you should pay more attention to the critical things that help you achieve success. If you spend more time on the things that give you more results, then you may see your productivity shoot up. So, what happens to the less critical or smaller stuff? Let it go!

You can also apply the Pareto principle to any aspect of your life. Marketers also apply the 80/20 rule. For marketing, 80% of marketing profits come from 20% of the customers. In human resources and employee relations, 80% of the most productive tasks come from 20% of the employees. For self-development and time management, 80% of your successes come from 20% of your efforts or actions.

For this reason, applying the 80/20 principle, you can scale up productivity in the areas that affect your bottom line. It will help you know how to assign tasks to employees and how to help them improve. It can also help you understand what areas to spend more time on and which to improve. For marketing, the Pareto principle can help you streamline your customer base to focus on serving the performing customers. Then, you can work out a strategy on how to convert the non-performing prospects or customers.

10 Bad Habits that Destroy Your Productivity

- Spending too much time on a single task, even when it can take less time.

- Sleeping through the morning hours instead of planning your day.

- Browsing the web without any clear cut plan.

- Not planning or prioritizing your day.

- Working for long stretches of hours, peering into your PC screen without taking a non-work related break.

- Maintaining unhealthy eating habits, like skipping meals or having the wrong diet.

- Waiting for years for the perfect time to start pursuing your goals.

- Making excuses for not pursuing or accomplishing your dreams.

- Only working on urgent tasks and leaving the important or non-urgent tasks undone.

- Leaving tasks until the last minute before executing them.

Chapter Summary

In chapter five, we have looked at the following concepts:

- Time is limited, but everyone has an equal amount of 24 hours daily.

- Successful people share the same number of hours as the less successful, but the differences lie in how the successful manage their time.

- Successful people create a schedule to help manage time effectively.

- Always break down tasks into smaller achievable pieces.

- Draw out your plans ahead, either in the evening before the close of work or morning before the start of work.

- Multitasking is not a sign of efficiency, but only helps in producing lower quality work.

- Avoid spending productive time on social media or emails as it can derail you from achieving your goals.

- Give yourself some non-work related breaks.

- Always buffer up your schedule, so you have short breaks of 25 minutes within each significant task.

- Practice the Pareto principle, or 80/20 rule that says 80% of your success will come from 20% of the effort you invest in it.

- Excessive sleep in the morning hours, spending too much time on a single task, and more, are some of the negative habits affecting your productivity level.

In the next chapter, you will learn about the three pillars of productivity you require to become a top performer.

CHAPTER SIX

THE 3 PILLARS OF PRODUCTIVITY YOU NEED TO UNLOCK YOUR FULL POTENTIAL

You have what it takes to be more productive and enjoy unlimited success. However, it will require a strong desire, decision, action, and a few productivity hacks to succeed. The TEA is a productivity framework that has the potential to move you closer to your goals. It will help you to manage your time, energy, and attention more effectively to overcome the challenges on your way to fulfilling your dreams.

A survey published in the New York Times showed that 81% of Americans have thoughts of writing a book. The study found out that if these people had pursued their dreams, at least 200 million books would have been written. However, only 80,000 people get around to writing and publishing their work annually. The above figure accounts for 0.4% of those who wish to publish their work. The remaining 81% only talk about their dream of writing a book.

What, in essence, actually stops most people from attaining their full potential in life? The simplest way to answer this question is with the TEA framework. The other answer is that those who excel at their craft make taking action on their goals a matter of habit, rather than something on their wish list. They commit to their goals, set a plan of action, and refuse to allow any excuse to stop them from achieving them. Successful people are die-hard doers and not procrastinators. You will become more productive when you learn how best to manage your time, attention, and energy. So, what is the TEA framework?

TEA: Three Obstacles Framework to Increased Productivity

Obstacles and challenges are real. These three simple categories explain the barriers people face in their pursuit:

- Time

- Energy

- Attention

The TEA framework is a powerful tool that helps individuals self-diagnose the hindrances to attaining their true potential. Once they are able to identify these challenges, then they can better focus on their most important tasks. Usually, such tasks are the ones that will have a massive impact on their bottom line.

Category 1: Energy & Attention, But No Time

Time is an essential factor for success, and anyone who must attain success must know how to manipulate time in their favor. However, those within this category possess the energy, desire, and passion to help them succeed. They believe they do not have enough time to get things done correctly. Thus, they develop the mentality of one who is stuck or trapped.

This feeling of inadequacy will cause those under this category to execute tasks haphazardly, delay tasks, or outright abandon their responsibilities. When you develop this type of mindset, here is how it reflects:

- There is so much to do and so little time to get things done.

- It would have been nice if time would extend beyond 24 hours.

- It appears that time always seems to run faster than ever.

The best way to describe people with no time, but more energy and attention is...overwhelmed. When you get to the point of feeling overwhelmed, if you do not tread with care, everything begins to scatter like a pack of cards. It is at this point when productivity starts to diminish.

Sometimes, it is not that you do not have enough time to get tasks done. It might be a case of not having a well-planned schedule or To-Do list. At other times, it could be that the person has procrastinated on the task until time has run out. Also, some people take on more responsibilities than they can handle. Instead of delegating part of the functions, they try to manage the situation themselves until things go awry. At other times, the jobs might, in reality, be bigger than the person can accomplish in the designated time frame. In this situation, the person requires a more realistic and flexible schedule to start and finish the task.

Other scenarios include an employee who gets to work quite early in the morning and does not return from work until late at night. Again, a supplier who makes too many trips daily, trying to deliver goods to clients at distant locations. A working-class mom with a 9 to 5 job, kids to cater to, and a degree to complete will most times feel overwhelmed. One thing is a common feature with all those mentioned above. They all have the energy to get things done and pay attention to their craft, but always feel overwhelmed due to limited time.

3 Components of Effective Time Management

Time does not exist in a vacuum but can be quantified. The quality of each second you use depends on whether or not it drives you closer to your goals. Therefore, time works best in the following situations:

Systems

Life is a combination of dependent and interdependent structures or systems. Each of these systems impact on the other in unique ways. Your ability to understand and manipulate or utilize these systems in accomplishing your goals will determine your level of success. For instance, technology can either help advance your course or serve as a distraction, depending on how you use it. The government and its agencies help create an enabling environment for businesses or individuals to thrive. However, if you get caught on the wrong side of the law, it can become your worst nightmare.

An organizational structure with the chains of command can help navigate business operations for success. When an organization or individual builds systems around their business operations, they increase their chances for success.

Strategies

A strategy is a tool used by highly successful people in enhancing their performance. It is a game plan, a compass, or a road map to getting to where you want to in your personal or business life. To win the battle of life, you need a strategy. Your strategy determines the kind of result you get from a given task or situation.

To succeed at anything, you must be willing to change your approach if the current one becomes a stumbling block to your progress. If checking your emails only distracts you from your critical tasks, then it may be a wise decision to restrict email viewing to a specific time.

People

Systems and strategies make it easier to accomplish your goals efficiently, but working with people is a different ball game. To excel, you must incorporate systems and strategies. How you go about relating with people will determine whether or not a strategy will work or fail.

Systems revolve around people as they will be the ones to implement them. To succeed in working with people, you require effective communication, teamwork, and the ability to delegate. You should be able to outsource, set expectations, provide an action plan, and give room for creativity. People work more effectively when they feel involved in a system, own the process, and can relate to it.

Strategies for Expanding Your Time

So, what can a person with motivation, but no time do? It's not likely you will be able to expand time, but these simple strategies can help you create ample time to get things done:

Schedule Daily Tasks on Your Calendar

Create a daily plan of all the tasks you need to accomplish, with a specific time for each. Have a calendar like the Personal Kanban board Google Calendar, or Outlook to help you schedule. In creating a daily plan remember to add buffer time to it. Also, break the responsibilities into smaller, manageable tasks. Do not overcrowd your table, but include time for family and friends in your program.

Follow through on your plans and avoid leaving things until the last minute.

Delegate Responsibilities

The fact is that you can only do as much as a single person can. Since you are not superhuman, you must rely on others to get things done from time to time. You need to learn the art of delegation and outsourcing where necessary.

Free Up Your Schedule

Some tasks on your To-Do list have been there for ages without any action being taken on them, but they are taking up valuable space for handling other meaningful tasks. When you free up your schedule, it gives you more space to complete critical tasks, while you allow others to handle the remaining ones. You might be an excellent worker, smart, and organized. However, if you spend the bulk of your time on the less essential tasks, you may be efficient, but not productive (effective) enough.

Create a System for Scheduling Time

Creating workable systems with timelines to get all tasks executed will help you spend quality time on essential jobs. You want to get more done, but that cannot possibly happen without assigning tasks to others. You must learn how to use what (time) you've got.

Effective time management goes beyond filling your day with work. It involves working in a simple, systematic, and timely manner, but also to know when to stop working. To excel at what you do, you must create a system or routine that works well and learn to stick to it.

Category 2: Possessing Time and Attention, But No Energy

When an individual lacks the energy to accomplish tasks, they begin to feel frustrated. They have the time and attention to complete the task but require steam or energy. A lack of energy can result in demotivation, procrastination, and more. Thus, such people end up not following through with their primary tasks. A burnt-out person sometimes says, 'I'm tired, weak, or exhausted and don't feel like doing anything.' Other times they say, 'I don't feel up to it.'

Scenarios of people with time and attention without energy include:

- A professor with groundbreaking research ideas, but who can't seem to put the pieces together to go public.

- The overall best marketing salesman (three years in a row) in your department who can't meet your marketing expectations anymore.

- Any employee who you can't seem to trust with handling bigger tasks.

"The key that unlocks energy is desire. It's also the key to a long and interesting life. If we expect to create any drive, any real force within ourselves, we have to get excited."-Earl Nightingale

You may have all the degrees in the world, purchase all the tools for working, but without the zest or energy, you are moving nowhere. When a person loses steam or becomes exhausted, even with adequate time and attention, they might find it near impossible to deliver efficiently still. It will take some adjustments to increase their productivity when energy levels drop.

Simple Strategies to Get an Energy Boost After a Decline

Public speaker Tony Swartz says, we all have the same number of hours per day, but each person's level of energy, quality, and quantity, depends on us.

The following ideas will help you boost your energy levels:

- Give yourself enough sleep instead of staying up late at night watching a movie. It will help you rejuvenate or regain your energy. Time remains 24 hours a day and has not once reduced or increased in human history. Your energy, on the other hand, does fluctuate. Energy levels can peak or drop fast, depending on cause and effect.

- Successful people understand the importance of conserving their energy. Expending all your energy on a task without taking time out to rest can lead to burnouts or low-quality work. Even if you assume you can still push yourself to work, you will end up with low quality work and become unmotivated.

- Read books that will help motivate you and give directions on how to stimulate growth. Reading suitable materials can help boost your energy levels by inspiring you or helping you to see what you do wrong. This book is an important go-to resource for discovering how to boost your energy. We shall discuss more on how to increase your energy in the next chapter.

- Take out time to exercise as it will help energize your body. Exercise can serve as a motivator.

- Break down big tasks into smaller, manageable ones and restrict yourself to a single task instead of multitasking.

- Take breaks from work often.

- Eating the right food combination can help increase your energy levels.

To remain productive, you must use your time wisely and channel your energy to completing the right tasks. Real progress doesn't come from trying to do so much, but in ensuring the little tasks you do turn out for the best.

Category 3: Time and Energy, But No Attention

Possessing a low attention span usually results in the feeling of being overwhelmed by any tasks one executes. Having a vibrant ability to pay attention goes beyond focusing on finishing tasks. The ability to focus or pay closer attention is what shapes life's major decisions and feats. Here are examples of statements made by people having issues with maintaining focus:

- Where do I start?

- There is so much to do, I don't even know where to start.

- Wow! How time flies!

- With a longer day, I could get more tasks done.

Sustained attention helps you achieve success on each job over time. Once you can single-task and not lose focus, then you are on your way to more significant achievements. Healthy attention requires the utilization of your time and energy toward achieving defined tasks successfully. The inability to focus or pay attention to what's important and not urgent will make all the difference.

Example of People With High Energy and Time, But No Attention

- A university professor who spends his time chatting with students instead of lecturing or conducting field research for seminar presentations.

- A person with a plan to set up a Non-Governmental Organization to cater to the needs of displaced persons, but ends up only talking without taking action.

- A music composer who spends most of his time writing songs without selling any or releasing a song to the public.

Simple Strategies to Increase Your Attention Level

A person with available time and the energy to do the work, but who cannot pay attention is said to be distracted. This is what you can do to boost attention level:

- Prepare your work station for the day's job by clearing your desk out.

- Before leaving for home today, create a plan or to-do list for tomorrow's task.

- Use the Personal Kanban board to help create a mental picture of what you want to achieve by the next day. It will help motivate and prepare your mind to single-task.

- Turn on 'Do Not Disturb' to minimize distractions once you intend on commencing a crucial task.

- Use the Pareto principle or 80/20 rule to focus your attention on the 20% of the efforts that help you succeed. Remember, 20% of the work effort produces 80% of the results you see.

- Focus — To increase your focus, you must work out ways of avoiding distractions.

- Goals — Find out what one skill you need to learn or one activity that can drive you closer to your goal. Create a plan of action and get to work implementing it.

- Mindset — Habits and belief systems can affect your productivity levels. Identify those traits that do not help you achieve your goals.

Chapter Summary

In this chapter, we discussed the following:

- Increasing your productivity does not happen by accident. It takes dedication, planning, and the TEA principles to excel.

- Time, Energy, and Attention are the three pillars to improved productivity.

- There are ten times more dreamers, or people who only talk about their goals, than there are those who take action on them.

- Highly productive people are die-hard doers, not dreamers or procrastinators.

- The TEA framework is a powerful tool to help you diagnose what hinders you from attaining your true potential.

- Some people have high energy, pay close attention, but have no time.

- If people with no time but energy and attention can learn to prioritize and manage their time effectively, they will become more productive.

- People who believe they do not have time, act like they are stuck or trapped. The best way to describe them is overwhelmed.

- Building systems, evolving strategies, and working effectively with people are the three great solutions to improving time efficiency.

- To use time effectively, you must organize, delegate, and unclog your schedule.

- Another category of people have time and pay attention, but do not have energy.

- People who have the time to carry out tasks and focus, but no energy to implement them, they get frustrated.

- The lack of energy can cause a loss of steam and lead to demotivation or procrastination.

- Adequate sleep, reading the right books, exercise, eating healthy, taking breaks from work, and breaking down tasks into smaller chunks will help regain your energy.

- Another category of people have time and energy to work, but no attention to detail.

- Possessing a low attention span can create a feeling of being overwhelmed.

- Focus and uninterrupted attention will help you excel in each task.

- Starting and finishing a task successfully will lead to effectiveness and efficiency.

- Systems and strategies are the building blocks of successful time management, but you require people to piece the puzzle together.

- It will help if you have a functional team to excel at any task.

- Communication, clear direction, and effective leadership are the tools for success and increased productivity.

- To help increase your attention level, remove things that cause distractions, like social media and email. Use 'Do Not Disturb' to remove distractions.

- Always work with a schedule and plan your next day's activities before leaving the office.

- Productivity is not about getting as much done as possible, but on finishing each job efficiently and effectively.

In the next chapter, you will learn about habits to increase your physical and mental energy.

CHAPTER SEVEN

HABITS TO INCREASE YOUR PHYSICAL AND MENTAL ENERGY

Your energy is the principal vehicle for bringing your dreams to reality. If given the opportunity, we all want to achieve our goals. Achieving one's goal is an integral part of human existence, but how many people truly achieve their life goals? How many have what it takes, even the physical and mental alertness required to see their goals to fruition? Many times people lack the will power, zest, or motivation to actualize their dreams. These deficiencies directly relate to each person's lack of physical and mental energy required to propel people into action.

The mind is one of the greatest tools each person possesses. To fully activate energies like confidence, happiness, focus, motivation, increased willpower, and productivity, the mind has to be in top gear. Your thought pattern affects your output and can sometimes determine how others see you. When you think happy thoughts, you become more content over time. When you are confident, it begins to reflect on your outward appearance.

If you must succeed in any endeavor, you need high mental energy, and often people discover, over time, that they lose steam and cannot get anything done anymore. What they lack is the required mental and physical energy to pursue their dreams. However, every ability evolves into a habit when people take the time necessary to study and acquire these habits. Mental and physical alertness is a function of certain habits people develop. If you see a person with low motivation, a lack of confidence, low physical and mental energy, sometimes it has to do with their habits. There are energy killing and energy-boosting habits, and the ones you subscribe to will determine how productive you can become.

"The first requisite for success is the ability to apply your physical and mental energies to one problem incessantly without growing weary."-Charles Caleb Colton

You need to inject new energies continuously into your life to remain balanced in your personal and career pursuits. But to make these new energies part of your DNA requires following a process, developing positive habits, and taking action always.

With that in mind, here are proven habits to set you on the right pedestal:

10 High-Powered Physical and Mental Energy Hacks

Tackle What You Dread the Most

Doing what you fear first gives you the confidence and energy to deal with other less critical jobs for the rest of your day. The first success provides motivation and an opportunity to exhale. Once you achieve success with the first task, it reduces the chance of procrastinating on other less critical tasks.

Visualize Before Bed

The thoughts you take to bed are essential in setting your mood for the next day. Nothing matters more than your state of mind just before you get into bed to sleep. It places you in the right frame of mind when you wake up. By visualizing possibilities before bed, you draw a direct connection between pleasure and waking up.

A positive mindset gives you all the energy you need to begin the day. It adds to the quality of your day and boosts your confidence level. This high energy can affect every other activity you get involved in over the course of the day.

However, visualizing works best when you have an action plan for each day and utilize your evening before to plan the next day's activities. This plan serves as a motivator.

Unclog Your Mind

It's true the never-ending things on the to-do list can leave a person feeling overwhelmed and the mind clogged. Also, with technology, the fast-paced world, deadlines, tons of email messages, appointments, and more, managing your day can become even more difficult.

To keep the mind free and mentally alert, delegate some tasks where necessary. Delegating to someone else relieves the stress level and reduces the volume of activity to worry about. Other activities, such as taking down notes, keeping a calendar, and setting reminders will help simplify your life.

Having a to-do list transfers work pressure from your mind to your schedule. It is a strategy that will help you unclog your mind and increase your mental energy. Also, it helps you focus more on a task without anxiety or a cluttered mind.

Getting the Right Amount of Sleep

Having the right amount of sleep per day has a direct correlation with your ability to function at optimal capacity. Sleep has a way of affecting the mental and physical state of an individual. The more sleep a person gets the more mentally alert they are, and vice versa.

Also, it helps to know your sweet spot, which is the right amount and the right kind of sleep you need. For some, too much sleep makes them groggy and exhausted. While some people might do well on six to seven hours of sleep, others might need eight hours or more to function fully.

Another point of note is the quality of sleep. Before retiring for the night you might need to turn off all devices that interrupt your sleep. Comfortable environments and the right kind of bedding can serve as a motivator for enhanced sleep. Other things that can boost the quality of sleep include:

- Taking a warm bath to relax the muscles.

- Reading a book in bed.

- Avoid screens two hours before bedtime.

- No caffeine after 3 P.M..

Spend a Good Chunk of Your Day Pursuing Your "Heart Project"

Heart projects are those specific things you pursue that center on your ultimate passion and goals. When you focus your energy on your passion and goals, it never seems like a task, but a hobby. Your heart project gives a new meaning to your life, making you very excited and revitalized.

Your passions give you something to always look forward to. They give you a reason to wake up daily and to hit the road with infectious enthusiasm.

Have a Sense of Gratitude

Starting the day with the right mental attitude gives a positive disposition to life. A good reminder of the things that are working in your life can help you approach the day in top gear. Try practicing being grateful always to enjoy greater mental energy. Be grateful for the things people take for granted, such as good health, a job, and the fact that you can earn a living salary. Be thankful for the relationships you have and all the seemingly small things that are currently working for you.

Remember that challenges are a part of life and tend to make you stronger. So, whatever challenge comes your way, look at things from the positive side. Everything cannot go down for you at the same time. A lifestyle of gratitude takes away boredom and reminds you of the most important things in life. Practice the act of writing down the things that are working in your life and focus more on them.

Have a Positive Outlook on Life

Being positive and optimistic about life is a great approach to boosting mental energy. You can replace a depressive feeling with positive thoughts to experience an energy boost. The state of your mental energy is a great determinant of your productivity levels. A negative disposition only causes a decline in your mental energy. Think positive thoughts and take advantage of opportunities as they present themselves.

Eat the Right Foods

The food we eat has a way of not only affecting our physical energy, but our mental energy as well. The saying 'you are what you eat' simply means you can draw energy from eating energy-giving foods by eating right. Food has a way of cramping our mental energy. For instance, carbohydrates turn sugar into fat in the body. This invariably weighs you down and leaves you feeling full and tired.

Eating unhealthy food leaves you with no nutritional value. Such foods decrease the overall wellbeing of the body and make you tired. A tired body automatically affects the mental state.

Adopt a plan to make helpful eating choices a lifestyle. Choose a diet that enhances mental alertness. Eating more calories earlier in the day than at night time will have a positive impact on your energy. Obesity is not one of the things you will want to add to your list of worries.

Healthy foods are rich in fiber, fruits and vegetables, protein, and other essential minerals that should be part of your diet to improve your energy. Also, water acts like magic to the body and it pays to stay hydrated all day long. However, drink water to stay hydrated, but do not allow water drinking to interfere with your work.

Get Inspired Through Exercise

Exercise is great for the brain, not only for weight control, but also to lower blood pressure. It can also help with depression and anxiety. Exercise boosts one's mood by kicking up your endorphin level, which is the 'feel-good' chemical in the body.

When involved in exercise, the heart rate increases and invariably decreases the stress level in the brain.

More benefits of exercise include:

- Better sleep

- Increase in self-esteem and self-confidence

- Brain boost

Stay Active but Enjoy It While on It

Sticking to exercise routines can be a near-impossible task for some people. However, besides the traditional jogging and brisk walk forms of exercise, you can find an enjoyable active method to keep your body functioning. Also, engaging in sports and hobbies is an excellent way to keep the body energized and the mind active.

Engaging Activities Include:

- Working out with friends

- Going for short walks

- Running

- Hiking

- Biking

- Dancing

- Skating

Surround Yourself With Happy People

Most people are naturally sociable, others are not, but relationships are an integral part of human existence. High energy, happy people carry the virus with them and if you stick long enough around them, you will become infected with happiness. They make you happy and full of energy.

Your relationships, therefore, will increase or decrease your energy level as you choose your associations. Ensure that you stay with people you enjoy being with.

Having a social network that aligns with your goals and needs can provide a kind of support group. Support groups can help increase your self-worth and reduce stress levels. Social gatherings are particularly useful for introverts who find interacting a little challenging. It allows them to express themselves, have fun, and laugh to serve as a boost.

Let Your Mind Travel in Meditation

Meditation involves deep thinking or using the power of imagination to recreate your world from what it is to what or where you desire it to be. Meditation helps you tap into the abilities of your mind to predict a better future through mental visualization. Successful people make use of meditation to find answers to even thorny issues.

The ultimate goal of meditation is inner peace and relaxation. Studies have shown that meditation (no matter how brief) is an excellent tool for reducing stress. Stress can have a toll on your physical or mental energy, and meditation can provide stress relief. Taking a couple of minutes daily o engage in mindful meditation will help ease most forms of stress and anxiety. Meditation is a useful tool in the fight for mental health and for fighting mental disorders.

Rejuvenate Your Body and Mind in a Yoga Session

Yoga has provided intrinsic value to humanity over the ages. It is a physical and mental exercise that helps rejuvenate the body and motivate the mind. Yoga combines postures, meditation, relaxation, and breathing techniques. There are a lot of benefits associated with yoga practice in the development of your physical and mental energy.

Yoga Benefits:

- Improves muscle strength – This protects against back pain and arthritis.

- Increases blood flow – Yoga releases energy in your body cells and aids blood circulation.

- Increases heart rate – Since Yoga involves physical exercise it causes rapid heart beating.

- Drops blood pressure and blood sugar.

- Makes focusing easier – Studies have shown that yoga practice improves coordination, memory, and IQ levels.

- Improves sleep.

- Reduces the fluctuation of the mind.

Get Into the Play Mood More Often

The saying that 'all work and no play makes Jack a dull boy' refers to the mental and physical state of wellbeing. Any activity that is fun and gives us joy or a childlike spark could be termed as play. Being busy with no time for fun activities or hobbies can have its toll on our energies. Play is different for every individual based on needs, interests, and wants. It doesn't necessarily have to be on your to-do list, but an activity you find fascinating. The fun activity could range from cooking, dancing, listening to music, going to the cinema, to field and track events — any hobby.

Create Routines

Creating energy-boosting habits as a part of your work or personal routine can help keep your energy levels high. Also, you can seek out small activities to boost energy fast while at work. Routines in sleeping habits, eating times, exercise, Yoga, a grateful attitude, and work activities can be very beneficial. Once you can master routines and it becomes a part of your life, then your productivity will go up.

Address Issues Head-On

Leaving issues on the front burner or unattended for long can have its toll on your energy levels, causing stress. Mental stress can drain your energy as much, if not more, than physical strain. Once you are mentally stressed, the first thing to do is to identify the triggers. The next thing to do is to begin devising strategies to tackle stress. Tackle them head-on and gain more energy for success.

Learning to increase your energy should be rather interesting. The use of substances should not be an option. Taking action is a vital aspect of finding your energy. Once you can make these practices a habit, they eventually become a lifestyle and more natural to achieve.

Chapter Summary

- Increasing your physical and mental energy requires deliberate actions that require incorporating them into your lifestyle.

- You need to inject fresh energy into your life regularly to enjoy a balanced flow of energy.

- Taking care of the tasks you dread the most will give you the energy and confidence to do more.

- Organize your thoughts by visualizing the job before you go to bed.

- Free your mind of overwhelming feelings and too many tasks.

- Sleep is important. Get enough of it.

- Your heart project is in the area of your passion and should be pursued with enthusiasm.

- Have an attitude of gratitude always.

- 'You are what you eat.' In other words, eat the right food with the proper nutritional value for your body.

- Engage in inspiring active or physical activities that you enjoy and your energy levels will go up.

- Socialize more by surrounding yourself with happy people.

- Happy people carry infectious energy.

- Meditation is a powerful energy booster.

- Practice yoga to improve your energy levels.

- You need to play more. The right type of play creates an exhilarating feeling.

- Get into regular habits that condition the mind for good.

- Take the bull by the horns when dealing with problems.

In the next chapter, you will learn how to get yourself motivated within a few minutes using science-backed tricks.

CHAPTER EIGHT

MOTIVATION IN MINUTES: SCIENCE-BACKED TRICKS

What keeps one going amid differing circumstances and challenges in life? When an idea does not seem to work, or one faces setbacks or failures, what gives you the courage to keep trying? Even when it isn't convenient, what causes you to rise early in the morning to meditate, study, do your routine exercises, or head to work?

The truth is that no genuine success can ever occur without motivation. Motivation is the driving force, just as fuel aids a vehicle's movement. Motivation is what gives wind to your sail, the driving force that keeps you going when everything else seems not to work. However, being motivated or staying motivated is not as easy as it looks. It tasks your physical and mental energy. When that happens, how do you remain motivated?

Here are some scientifically proven ways to get you focused and motivated for increased productivity within minutes:

Boost Your Confidence With a High-Power Pose

The Required Length of Time: 2 Minutes

Your body language is a central factor in how others perceive you. It also affects your internal body chemistry. The way you carry yourself and perform certain activities, your posture, movements, and more send positive or negative vibes to others. Amy Cuddy from Harvard says that "our nonverbals govern how other people think and feel about us."

Research from Princeton, Harvard, and other institutions point to how body language can affect interactions in the workplace. Using the right words can help pass the right message. However, body language can influence the meanings you read into any message.

Therefore, just as body language affects a message, so does it affect your motivation level. Professor Amy Cuddy of Harvard School of Business, speaking on body language, says that the power pose provides another channel for communicating non-verbally. The way you carry your body can say a lot about you as well as affect your productivity levels. Your body language, postures, and carriage can tell a lot about you.

What's a Power Pose?

There are two known kinds of power poses, which are the high and low power pose. High power pose deals with positioning your body in an open instead of a slouched or hunched position, even if seating or standing. In a high power pose, you keep your chest and arms spread open and avoid staying in a slouched position.

Hence, researchers identify that maintaining a high-power pose can increase your testosterone levels, a hormone responsible for a confidence boost. The high-power posture, also in the process, reduces cortisol levels, which are responsible for increasing stress in the body.

However, in a lower power-pose, the individual slouches in a position that makes you appear small or bunched up.

Therefore, to give yourself the needed mental boost, try out simple high power poses and see the effect on your productivity levels. Always consciously stand or sit in a high power pose manner. A study at Princeton shows that body language carries more expressions than just facial.

Remember to actively, not passively, communicate and align your entire body facing the other person when talking with them. Smile often, as research also confirms that smiling can boost your confidence level too.

Give Yourself a Fresh Start

The Required Length of Time: 3-5 Minutes

Most people make resolutions, particularly at the beginning of the year, and this helps serve as a source of motivation. By making resolutions, you give yourself a chance to start anew. It can also create a burst of energy to accomplish more tasks, according to a study conducted by the Wharton School of Business.

A publication by the Institute of Operations Research and Management Science identified that the use of salient temporal landmarks helps people in attaining their goals. They develop the willpower to tackle any task when they decide to make a fresh start. Such fresh starts occur during temporal landmarks like their birthdays, a new week, a month or year, holidays, a new semester, or session. Using Google search, the team identified some areas requiring a fresh start to include dieting, visiting the gym, and committing to achieving goals.

To make a fresh start, using landmarks, people can move on from past imperfections to pursue bigger goals that will impact their lives. In other words, the decision to make a fresh start could serve as a source of motivation leading to a change in behavior and increased productivity.

How Do You Get a Fresh Start in Life

Everyone has past and recurrent events in their lives. Some of these events can push one closer or farther from achieving their goals. However a critical look at those events or occurrences can turn into a fresh start. You can set a negative or positive situation into an avenue for a fresh start. For example, a recent loss of a job, break up, graduation, or relocation to a new community can serve as motivation to start that business you have been saving for or longing to set up.

Temporal landmarks help you disconnect from past failures and make a concrete plan on how to advance your goals. To help inspire you to succeed you need to take the next step, which is to write down your goals. Create a plan of action or to-do list to channel your new-found energy in achieving your goals. Also, having a fresh start does not have to be limited to the beginning of the year, but at any time you discover the need to re-define a situation or occurrence.

Indulge Yourself a Little With a Treat of Chocolates

The Required Length of Time: 1 Minute

Eating chocolates might appear bad for your teeth or too sugary for you. However, chocolate can have powerful motivational benefits. Chocolate contains dopamine-releasing properties with chemical reactions known to produce these chocolate effects on your brain:

- Dopamine causes an increase in the heart rate leading to higher motivation.

- Eating chocolate releases serotonin and phenylethylamine into your bloodstream. Serotonin is a neuro-transmitter and can help calm your nerves, while phenylethylamine promotes stimulation. White chocolate contains more of the two properties and offers more value. Dark chocolate contains antioxidants that help slow down cognitive decline and increase your concentration level.

- Chocolate works as a mild form of antidepressant. When you consume chocolate, it causes a chemical reaction in the brain that stimulates a feeling of bliss, a 'feel-good sensation,' and motivation.

Build Your Brain Power With Healthy Foods

Eating healthy will have a direct impact on your overall health. Your health is the only guarantee of enjoying wealth when you finally become successful. However, to successfully set, pursue, and achieve your goals you need your health.

Certain classes of food only help to slow down your mental and physical development as well as to make you ill. Your body needs the right amount of nutrients to rebuild or repair worn tissues. When you give it the right food, it can not only provide the energy to do work, but also boosts your brain development.

What Foods Can Boost Your Brainpower?

There are a lot of foods that, once eaten, can serve as fuel for the body in helping you reach your goals. Examples of motivating foods include foods rich in protein, healthy fats and oils, fruits and vegetables, nuts and seeds, whole grains and more.

Foods rich in Vitamin B serve as a stimulant and can help increase your energy levels, motivation, and brainpower. For instance, Vitamin B contains dopamine responsible for giving you a motivated feeling. You can get a good dosage of Vitamin B in turkey, salmon, tofu, bananas, spinach, hazelnuts, walnuts, and avocado pear. However, foods with high cholesterol and fatty foods are not so healthy or helpful for brain development.

Fish like salmon, containing oils and Omega 3 fatty acids can aid speedy brain development. It can also protect against memory loss and dementia. Besides chocolates, nuts and seeds also slow down cognitive decline. Other fruits and vegetables that contain dopamine properties include spirulina, blueberries, etc.. Studies show that avocado pear contains properties that fight the free radicals responsible for cell damage, reduce the progress of Alzheimer's disease and dementia. Avocado pear is an excellent food for building muscle function and learning development.

Spend Time in Nature

Nature has a unique way of connecting with the human sweet spot. It can motivate you even in the worst of situations and the most unlikely circumstances. It's so easy to get trapped in the madness of earning a living and pursuing set goals that you forget to enjoy even the little you've earned. You sometimes forget to take time out to enjoy even the gifts of nature.

"In the depth of winter, I finally learned that there was in me an invincible summer"-Albert Camus

One of the best ways to get motivated in minutes is to allow nature to slip through your being. Spending more time in nature will not only help you to unwind, but also inspire you to crack hard-nut work issues. So, what can you do?

Take a walk

Walking acts like medicine to the body and the human psyche. Instead of driving or possibly take a taxi, bus, or train, can you take a walk home? Or at least stop a few meters from the nearest bus stop and walk the remaining way home. Several things normally occur when you take a walk. It gives you time to reflect on the activities of the day, weeks, and months. You can also meditate on nutty issues at work, and because it is a different environment, you don't feel choked.

You can also take a walk on the beach. Walk on your bare feet, the waves to the left, trees to the right, music from a distance, other fun-seekers running around, screams, and excitement in the air. Just sipping in the cool summer wind can do much magic to your soul. As you ponder on the issues of life, your goals, work, and personal life, it won't take long to get a burst of energy coming in.

Go On a Vacation

A trip to some of those places you have always dreamed of can create the needed motivation you seek. There are dozens of exciting and exotic locations, natural reserves, game reserves, and waterparks to explore. Besides the wonderful sites to see, merely being in the green will give you a usual volume of motivation and energy.

Research from the University of Essex shows that colors communicate tones, moods, and feelings to people. The color green is said in two different studies to serve as a motivator, while sparks of green can boost your creativity levels. Hence, surrounding your office or room with a touch of green should do wonders for your energy.

For example, Andrew is a guy who likes creating his to-do list for the next day when he is getting ready for bed. He looks through the activities of the day, successes, failures, uncompleted tasks, and more, and then schedules them into the next day's activities. Once Andrew completes this task, he lays on his bed and then tries to visualize... *What will tomorrow look like?* he asks himself. *What do I want to achieve for tomorrow? What problems do I have to surmount in my work and personal life tomorrow to achieve my goals?* After some time, he puts out the reading lamp and rests for the night. When morning comes, Andrew is pumped up, excited about the day's activities and can't wait to hit the ground running

Research confirms that people respond differently to situations, and that helps to motivate them. Science identifies that there are two types of motivation, intrinsic (internal) and extrinsic (external). For instance, when you clean your home just when you are expecting some friends to come to isit, that's external motivation. Extrinsic motivation depends on something xternal or from your environment to stimulate a course of action. Belle ooper, says extrinsic motivation can be summed up using conditional tatements, such as 'if,' followed by a reward. For example, 'if you can hit target of five sales consistently in the next three months, you will qualify or Regional Marketing Manager.' That's an external incentive for getting task done. Rewards tend to narrow the thinking processes to succeed.

However, researchers at Princeton identify that such a reward system or external motivation, over time, leads to poor performance. Tasks nvolving innovation and creativity produce higher performance when there s internal motivation. For instance, staying after close to work on your kills in order to improve upon something is intrinsic motivation. Intrinsic notivation is part of what promotes creative works. Your goal is the notivating factor.

Elements of Intrinsic Motivation

Dan Pink talked about the three elements of intrinsic motivation:

- Autonomy

- Mastery

- Purpose

Autonomy

Autonomy deals with making choices. When you have a sense of wnership or feel you are in control of your choices, it gives you intrinsic notivation. Such a person can look at all possibilities creatively to get the task done. As such, having areas within your control on a job will give you some level of motivation about it. For example, your boss gives you a project to execute. If you have room to make some decisions on the structure, progress, and delivery date of the tasks, it becomes easier to feel motivated than if you only have to do as instructed. So, seeking ways to increase your autonomy on a task will naturally lead to motivation as you can own the process.

Mastery

When you love what you do it helps you get better at it, even without external motivation. You will be willing to develop yourself to get better at your task when it matters to you, not just to the company, and when areas requiring your skills come up, you will feel excited and motivated to use your skills.

Purpose

When you feel like a project or task is something bigger than your personal interests, then your focus is on purpose. Motivation becomes intrinsic when the individual's focus in on the benefit, such as how a task will add to society or benefit the company's customers. You become motivated when you see the actual value a project will add to customers and others.

Chapter Summary

In this chapter, we have discussed the following ideas extensively:

- Challenges are some of the hallmarks of pursuing any worthwhile goal in life. People somehow find the motivation to pursue their dreams despite their obstacles.

- Motivation is what causes someone to rise early each day to pursue a dream, even after setbacks and failures.

- Motivation comes from internal (intrinsic) and external (extrinsic) sources.

- High power poses help inspire you to keep working.

- Your body language says a lot about you and can affect your motivation levels.

- Seating or standing in a slouching or hunched position is a low power pose, and it can affect your motivation at work or in an interview.

- Seating or standing in an open or upright position with squared shoulders facing ahead is called high power pose. It can help boost your energy levels and increase motivation in the space of two minutes.

- Making a fresh start in life can serve as a motivator.

- People make weekly, monthly, and yearly resolutions. Other resolutions come during their birthdays, after a loss of a job, or a breakup. This temporal landmark system serves as motivation to either stop or start doing certain things.

- Indulge yourself a little by eating white, brown, or dark chocolate as it contains dopamine, which is one of the feel-good ingredients for motivation.

- Eating foods rich in protein, oils, omega 3 fatty acids, seeds, and nuts, etc. can help boost your energy levels and motivation.

- Staying locked up indoors or all week in the office is enough to kill motivation. Taking a trip with mother nature can stir up something in you. Take a walk, go to the beach, and let these things inspire you.

- You can get motivated or feel a sense of autonomy when you feel like you can own the process or have played a significant role in the decision-making process of a task.

- Mastering the process of getting things done within your organization can serve as a substantial boost for you. Once you enjoy doing what you do, if need be, you can study more to hone your skills.

- It can work with a purpose, such as for the overall good or benefit of others, it tends to serve as a drive to continue on a mission. Knowing how much value or impact you have on customers and humanity can create motivation.

In the next chapter, you will learn about the secret to increased efficiency and focus using the Pomodoro method.

CHAPTER NINE

THE POMODORO METHOD — THE SECRET TO INCREASED EFFICIENCY AND FOCUS

There are so many tasks to accomplish every day, and it seems like there is never enough time. You have tight deadlines, but no time to get everything done. Now, it may have gotten so bad you constantly have to take work home so that you can meet your target deadlines. During some weeks, everything goes smoothly, and you hit your target. On others, it's a struggle. And it's all adding up, making you more and more frustrated. You are beginning to lose steam. So, what do you do in such situations?

A lot of people struggle with maintaining focus at work. Sometimes, people sit all day at their desks but still end up achieving little due to lack of concentration, fatigue, or the lack of motivation. The secret ingredient you need is the Pomodoro method for better focus and efficiency.

When I first heard about the Pomodoro technique, my interest peaked immediately. Being a life coach, however, it took some time before I could find time in my schedule to study the Pomodoro technique and to give it a shot for myself. I had heard a lot about the value of the method and was eager to try it out and, to say the least, the result on my productivity level was phenomenal. If you are struggling with maintaining your focus and efficiency at work, this is just the right tool to try: the Pomodoro method.

What Is the Pomodoro Method?

The Pomodoro method is a time management tool to help increase your efficiency and focus at work. There is hardly ever enough time to get everything done. With this in mind, the Pomodoro technique teaches you to work with the available time on your hands. Instead of racing against time, Pomodoro encourages you to streamline by structuring your time into 25 minute and 5 minute segments.

In other words, you break your workday into smaller chunks of 25 minutes and 5 minutes. The 25 minutes go into accomplishing parts of your tasks, while the 5 minutes are for short breaks. This is known as the Pomodoro method. However, after about four intervals, or Pomodoros, then you can extend the break to 15 to 20 minutes.

What's the Value in the Pomodoro Technique?

The Pomodoro design helps you focus on what is most important daily. Sometimes, we carry on work with the impression that we have enough time to get the day's job done. Then, we allow distractions to get in our way. An urgent email comes in from a friend, and then you think, 'Message from John... Okay, let me quickly reply to the email...", and you suspend your current task at hand. Before you know it, you're caught up in other distracting tasks, and half of the day goes by without accomplishing much. Once the deadline is just two days away, then you're in a frenzy, trying to squeeze everything in so you can deliver on time.

126

The Pomodoro technique provides an immediate sense of urgency about your work. It helps you focus even if it is only for 25 minutes on your most important tasks. After 25 minutes, you can allow yourself some distractions before getting back to work on the same tasks. The argument is that, once you have the discipline to follow through on this formula, at the end of each day, you will have increased your productivity astronomically. So, instead of squandering time on distractions, you focus your time on your key tasks.

If you invest in intervals of 25 minutes for tasks, with 5 minutes for breaks, for 12 times in a single day, you will have worked for 300 minutes by the end of the day. If you add up 5 minutes times 12, that's 60 minutes, which results in at least 7 hours of work in a day. You still have at least one hour for a break, assuming you work 8 hours per day or a 9 to 5 job.

The Pomodoro technique helps increase your productivity by cutting down on distractions and getting more tasks done. The forced breaks take away the daily fatigue or burnt-out feeling at the end of work. In addition, it's unhealthy to spend endless hours cranking at your desk, hoping to get more tasks done. Forcing yourself to work with the Pomodoro method helps you to achieve more while keeping your energy levels high.

From an evolutionary biology point of view, the human brain should not work under so much undue pressure at a stretch. Although the brain can withstand the stress (after all, it can handle extremely complex pressures), over the years, the effect of the strain will likely show on your health. The human brain helps you survive any situation, but cannot stay focused on one task for so long without a drop in concentration. Therefore, using a simple technique, such as Pomodoros, your brain can enjoy an energy boost, constant alertness, and an increase in the quality of work produced.

Strategies to Make the Pomodoro Technique Work for You

Not everyone has the same work schedule or nature of work. Because of this, you can tailor the Pomodoro technique to suit your unique circumstances. For instance, a person in marketing, engineering fieldwork or a writer or journalist, will have a different working environment.

Initially, using such incessant breaks will appear awkward and unnatural. I must confess, it is a cumbersome experience when you start micro-managing tasks with a timer. In fact, at first, I had several shifts from 25 to 45 minutes so that I could cater to some urgent issues. At other times, I had to attend to a prospective client with large accounts and altered the setup. Also, I had meetings with clients during the day, training sessions, and all of that to deal with. Under such circumstances, I had to turn off the Pomodoro timer to get other things done.

However, to help achieve my goal, I had incorporated the Pomodoro technique with the personal Kanban board. On days where I had to work more from the office or at the desk, I used more of the Pomodoro method. It helped me to get things organized faster and more efficiently. On such days when I have meetings with staff or personal coaching sessions with clients, I suspended the Pomodoros, as I can't make others leave with the 25 minutes to 5 minutes schedule. Still, incorporating the Pomodoro technique this way, I experienced an exponential increase in productivity levels. I helped me single task better and got more done faster.

Here is how the Pomodoro method can work for you:

Work With a Stopwatch or Timer App

Since you must create a timestamp, a stopwatch or app will serve as the best way to set the 25-minute intervals. There's no way to discipline yourself to the Pomodoro method without a timer. Checking the time manually will result in more disappointment than success. Besides, once you get caught up with work, you are bound to forget your timing.

You can download the Pomodoro Timer app from the iTunes store for Apple users. Or try ClearFocus for Android users.

Single Task, Not Multitasking

It should be clear by now the dangers and disadvantages of multitasking. To increase your productivity, try to single-task by assigning only one task to a 25-minute interval. If you need more than a single 25 minutes to get that task done, then use as many 25 minute intervals as possible, but be sure not to spend more time than a single task should take normally.

Be Committed

As much as you want to be flexible, it will help if you stick to the Pomodoro technique to get the maximum benefits. It's often tempting to skip the breaks and to keep working, especially when there are tight deadlines to meet. However, you must stick to your breaks, just as you stick to the task intervals.

Set Daily Goals

Like we already talked about, set daily goals in line with the tasks for that day. Each day's task should be specific to 25 minutes of work time and 5-minute breaks. Use as many as 25 minutes and 5-minute breaks as the day's activities will allow. Extend the breaks from 5 minutes to 15 minutes after the first four intervals of 5-minute breaks.

Stay Focused on Work

There are bound to be interruptions and other urgent or emergency issues. However, you must make it a habit to concentrate on your work for every 25 minutes and use the 5 minutes breaks as designated. The moment you allow interruptions to come into your day, others will use the excuse to disturb you. You will end up achieving little if there is too much interference.

Delay Email Reading and Social Media Distractions

Just because emails form a part of your work activities, does not mean you can allow email interruptions. Do not check your emails when taking care of a specific 25-minute task or during the 5-minute breaks. The 5-minute breaks are for non-work related activities that allow you some time to rejuvenate. If you spend 5 minutes on any work at all, that means you did not give your brain any time off.

There should be a specific time in your daily schedule for handling emails. You can have email reading come up two to three times in a regular work schedule. This will help in avoiding email or social media interruptions during crucial work time.

Enjoy Your Breaks

Since the 5-minute break intervals are not for working, what should you do with them? Five minutes is not a lot of time. Use your breaks to concentrate on non-work related activities. That's the only way you will be physically and mentally alert after the break. The reason the break is not more than 5 minutes is so that your body does not adjust to the resting period and get out of the work mode.

To use the 5 minutes effectively, you can get up from your work station and take a walk or grab a cup of coffee. Walking helps relieve body tension, as well as to loosen your muscles. Taking a deep breath to fill your lungs with oxygen offers a lot of benefits to your brain and the body. The oxygen released into the brain serves as a boost that can help you maintain focus. A more relaxed body makes it easy to work more efficiently and invariably get more quality tasks done daily.

In a nutshell, I started out testing the Pomodoro technique and ended up advocating this method to my clients. From personal experience, I concluded that the Pomodoro method might not fit into everyone's work schedule or lifestyle. One could, however, adopt the formula in resolving different work-related situations. The benefit for me is that using the Pomodoro technique on office and desk-related tasks helps me to be more productive.

Other Time-Tested Strategies to Improve Focus and Efficiency

Define Your Goal Clearly

If you must reduce distractions and focus your energy, then you need to state your goals clearly by writing them down. The value of a clearly stated goal is that it forces you to focus or concentrate on what truly matters to your work. If you do not have your goals stated, it will be more challenging to utilize the Pomodoro method. It will be best if you have defined goals to plan the structure of 25 minutes and 5-minute breaks.

Also, stating your goals makes it possible to build mental blocks. You can visualize the process to get tasks done and possibly see what it will look like once completed. When stating your goals, remember to write down what you intend to achieve through that goal and why. These last points help to motivate you toward pursuing the goals.

Take Your Time

It sometimes appears as if you are not hardworking when you take things slowly, but it's not true. Success is not a one-meter dash or a journey; it's a destination. Success is where you want to be, and everyone goes at their own pace. Working at a defined pace gives you the feeling of being in control and not overwhelmed. When working on tasks that require a lot of mental energy, working simply is a discipline that you must learn. Working at a defined pace allows you to pay attention to critical details, and that's how you should structure your tasks into the Pomodoro technique. At such a pace, you will be racing for quality content and not against time.

Can You Do It Now?

Some tasks appear hectic, and you may be tempted to leave them for later. However, you end up not doing them at all or waiting until it becomes urgent and important. When you leave a task until the last minute, it adds more mental pressure to your brain. Research shows that at least 15% of dults procrastinate what they need to do. Procrastination can drain you of motivation and give you the feeling that there is so much to do and so little time to get things done. This feeling can hurt the quality of your work. Procrastination can, over time, become a habit that results in low self-esteem. However, you can keep this in check by giving yourself strict deadlines, breaking the tasks into bite-sized chunks, and planning in advance.

A strategy that can help against procrastination is using the two-minute rule. With it, any job that only requires about two minutes to complete, you do immediately. Do not allow such tasks to add to the list of unfinished jobs. Some of these activities include sending an email or clearing out your desk. However, make sure everything is planned in your to-do list.

Join the 5 a.m. Club

Remember Robin Sharma's 5 A.M. Club? You can go back to chapter two to read more about it. However, rising early in the morning to plan your day, and getting into shape will make it easier to get the best out of the Pomodoro method. Using the 20/20/20 formula can help you to plan your day, get enough exercise, and meditate on what will help you succeed today. This should help you to relax and become more productive, giving you the needed boost to take charge of your day.

Conducive Environment

An unfriendly work environment kills motivation and can cause loss of concentration. Make your work environment less hostile, more inviting, and comfortable. Things such as the color of the office, furniture, and curtains can set the mood for work. Color communicates sadness, happiness, and excitement. Usually, brighter colors like green work best for motivation. The same goes for lighting. A poorly lit environment can cause a strain on the eyes. Lighting can also set the mood for a lively or melancholi atmosphere.

Take note of the sitting arrangement in the office, as a clumsy sitting arrangement can also affect focus. An overcrowded office will cause distraction and inconvenience. Ventilation and access to utilities, such a the restroom, etc. help you to concentrate better. Music can also help improve concentration. Music can encourage pleasant emotions and thoughts. It can also stimulate the mind, as well as help you to relax. Music can also help to channel your thoughts and overcome other subconsciou distractions. However, the choice of music will determine the value you get. Music with lyrics, however, may give you too much to think about and further create a distraction. As such, instrumental music often improve concentration more effectively.

Delegate Tasks

We shall discuss more on delegation in the next chapter. However delegation helps share the responsibility and increases your capacity to do more. It can also help you to become more efficient, while improving the quality of your work. Delegation also enhances creativity and flexibility, a more hands may mean better ideas on how to achieve a task.

The intrinsic value in the Pomodoro method is the ability to get mor done in as little time as possible, while maintaining your concentratio level. Therefore, schedule work time and break time accordingly. To exce

134

at any innovative idea, including the Pomodoro method, will take cooperation and discipline. No one can help you achieve success if you don't give it a shot.

Chapter Summary

- The feeling of 'so many tasks and so little time to get them done' can result in a drop in concentration.

- The Pomodoro method is a time management tool that helps you focus your energy on accomplishing the critical tasks, increasing concentration and productivity.

- The technique works by splitting your work time into 25 minutes of serious and focused work and 5-minute breaks.

- With carefully planned tasks, you can attain at least 25 minutes of work with 5-minute breaks, 8 to 12 times in a day.

- The Pomodoro technique helps you break the day's tasks into smaller manageable bits of 25 minutes to help you concentrate better.

- It enables you to reduce distractions or to not focus on less important tasks during critical work hours.

- The use of a Pomodoro timer or stopwatch, as well as mono-tasking instead of multitasking, is a powerful Pomodoro strategy to improve productivity.

- Set daily goals and follow through to increase productivity.

- Your 5-minute breaks should only be used to relax and not to focus on work.

- To succeed with the Pomodoro method, you must commit to a plan, avoid procrastinating, and delegate where necessary.

In the next chapter, you will learn about how to delegate effectively to get more tasks done and to increase productivity.

CHAPTER TEN

HOW TO DELEGATE TASKS

Some schools of thought state that 'if you want something done right, you do it yourself.` However, even though it makes sense to get things done yourself, the big question is, how much can a single person really achieve alone? When emperor Napoleon Bonaparte established the above statement, probably what he had in mind was the need to create structures and strategies at management levels so that execution of tasks would go smoothly. I came to this conclusion because Napoleon was a great French leader and Emperor. He rose to power during the French Revolution in the 1770s and championed the conquest of significant portions of Europe. If he meant the execution of tasks without the help of others, I doubt that the great Emperor would have been victorious at war as he had to work with his cabinet, generals, and a large troop of soldiers to succeed.

Delegation is a useful management tool for the success of personal and corporate goals. However, it's easy to delegate too little or too much to any given task. To strike a balance, knowing how to delegate is crucial.

As a critical skill, it is expedient that managers learn to delegate or outsource projects or tasks. Delegation saves a lot of time, reduces the workload, and allocates enough time for more important responsibilities.

When you assign jobs to qualified or experienced subordinates (freelance or in-house), it enhances productivity. Investing in training for in-house personnel is valuable as well.

What Is Delegation?

A delegation is an act of conferring authority or power on others to act on your behalf to carry out tasks. When delegating, you assign responsibilities to subordinates with specific terms of reference for the execution of such tasks. Meanwhile, while the responsibility lies on the staff to carry out the job, the superior must ensure proper communication, understanding, and adherence to standards and deadlines. This is the ability to recognize and convert the talents of team members for managerial goals. A high level of productivity is a reward for delegation. The workflow becomes smoother and less stressful when you delegate.

Reasons Managers Don't Delegate

Loss of Authority

Some managers find it difficult to delegate because they feel they are relegating their authority to someone else. Most people see delegation as a sign of weakness or think that the other person will do a shoddy job. However, letting others take up responsibility does not evoke fragility, but your ability to trust others. It also helps you see how well you can duplicate your strength in others by communicating effectively or through training. Delegation is a tool used by highly effective managers.

No One Does It Better

Another myth or misconception about delegation is that no other person can do better than you, but the truth is, delegation, most times, it brings creativity and different points of view to a project.

Delays in the Delivery of the Task

Again, some people hold the view that delegating a job will result in delays. It's true, you do need to bring subordinates up to speed before they can execute a task adequately, but how much can a manager achieve alone? Some of these issues can be resolved with proper staff training. Working alone limits your capacity to executive more jobs. There is so little a single person can achieve, but together, a team will get more done. Delegation not only helps to duplicate the effort and save time, but it also increases the quality of the work delivered.

Why Managers Delegate

The bulk always stops at the manager's table. This phenomenon creates some level of panic and dissuades people from delegating. However, the question for most leaders is: how should I delegate? When you delegate, you do not lose, but share your authority so that you can get more done.

A business has several important aspects to its functions. Marketing, sales, production, distribution, coordination of staff, and more, make up what managers face daily. The only way to successfully execute these roles is to allow others to work with you, while you focus on the strategy of the business. No business can excel where the manager buries himself in the daily operations of each unit. The manager needs to entrust unto faithful stewards parts of his or her powers while concentrating on strategies for expanding the business. Managers can focus on the bigger picture when they learn to delegate.

Increased Capacity

When a manager becomes overwhelmed beyond his ability, devising a system for sharing the work is the smartest thing to do. Why spend three months scrambling between six tasks when you could assign two teams or four individuals to carry on with it? The fear of losing quality or missing deadlines will, over time, result in lower quality work and more issues with deadlines. When the management team doesn't delegate, they experience more burn-outs than are necessary.

More Reasons to Delegate Tasks:

- The decision-making process and chain of command becomes more visible and operational with delegation. It also helps create a stronger and improved pool of talents amongst the team. Through assigning powers, others can develop better communication skills, sufficient motivation, supervision/guidance, and leadership traits.

- Delegation makes the superior-subordinate relationship more meaningful and recognizable. The authority or power can easily flow from the top to the bottom in an organization. With this recognized hierarchy, results are quite achievable.

- Delegation to both subordinates and superiors can bring about the expansion of the organization. This invariably will lead to creating more managerial roles and possibly the need for more outlets. It is an essential factor for an organization looking forward to horizontal or virtual growth; this is a plus.

- Effective delegation can help subordinates flourish and own the process. Subordinates no longer feel like just a number, but are more at the center of events. They are motivated to work because they have this feeling of importance in what they do. Every cadre of management can receive some form of job satisfaction, which further leads to stability and healthy relationships.

- Delegation of responsibility keeps you abreast of your work and puts the manager in the position of a distribution system or powerhouse rather than as a reservoir. The more you allow teams to develop, the more confident they will become. The more confidence other team members have, the more efficient and productive they will be. In the end, it will result in an improvement in the quality of work done in the organization.

- Delegation provides managerial training for subordinates. It is a vital tool for effective planning, development, and for encouraging promotion. It allows everyone to gain experience and grow on the job.

Simple Hacks to Delegating

For delegation to work effectively, it must be systematic and procedural, with timelines, checks, and balances. It doesn't just involve assigning duties and responsibility, but works best if you have a mastery of delegation methods. Delegation is a skill that requires training. Reading books, such as this one, can provide insight into delegation. Here are some simple steps to delegation:

Determine the Duties You Want to Delegate

The first step in delegation is to decide what jobs and responsibilities you wish to assign to members of the team. Break tasks into smaller units as a way of ensuring a good understanding of the objective. For instance, little jobs like flight bookings, scheduling meetings, or responding to emails should form part of the job responsibilities of an assistant. Some of such logistics might appear not to take much time, but there are more productive uses of your time.

Decide on the job in the list that suits you best and those that would be done better by someone else. You might not be skilled in certain areas, and doing the task takes a lot of time. Delegating such a responsibility to a person better equipped than you is ideal, provided they have a clear understanding of your instructions. There are some tasks that require your attention personally, but to help you plan, you can assign tasks based on the job description, roles in the office, or designation. Where you have senior, mid-level managers, and junior staff, you can assign tasks based on the level of authority and attention required. You can also use individual strengths and skills to decide what job to attach to other employees.

Consider Time Constraints

Delegating gives you more time to focus on the bigger picture. It enables you to focus on the intricacies of the business and the strategies required for reaching the company's goal. In assigning tasks, not all members of your team can deliver jobs as quickly as you might expect them to. This action might have to do with their wiring or strength in specific areas. Therefore, as a manager or team lead, you need to understand the depth of team members in deciding who takes on what.

Remember, the purpose of delegation is a smooth workflow. You don't want to miss a deadline or become overworked. Irrespective of the fact that you are better at managing tasks, time might not be on your side. The time-sensitive project should go to fast and capable hands on the team.

Determine Who You Will Delegate Each Task To

It is essential to know the strengths and weaknesses of everyone on the team. This will help you determine what responsibility to delegate to each personnel. From the list of prepared tasks, match each person with a job based on their strength.

Critically looking at their skill set or personality makeup can give you a clue as to who should handle a task. To delegate a job that requires teamwork to a single person, because he is a highflyer, might not always turn out right. Giving the role of team lead to a person who doesn't like teamwork sometimes might de-motivate or slow work progress. In some situations, solo-players learn to become team players and great leaders once they get the opportunity. Also, some other people do better when they work in a team than when working solo. It is your duty as a manager to spot and harness the values in personnel.

Sometimes, for flexible tasks, allowing people to select what project to execute might also help in achieving more significant successes at work.

When people can own a project, they feel better motivated to work. Most times, people select projects that they love or have a passion for and will likely achieve outstanding results.

Be Fair in Your Delegation

When assigning tasks, express confidence in your subordinate's abilities, but delegate objectively. Set a timeline from the outset of the project to avoid badgering them while they make progress. Incessant interference can put the team on edge or come off as a lack of confidence in their ability. Allow the unit to tackle problems on their own. After all, what's the point in delegating responsibility if you are going to micromanage them?

From the outset, be clear about your expectations, and be detailed with instructions. Specify the goals, vision, and milestones you want them to achieve. If they miss out on something vital, explain it to them again. Make them understand that you trust them and want to see them grow. Once they feel you are counting on them, they are more likely to deliver.

In the words of Jeffrey Pfeffer, the Thomas D. Dee II Professor of Organizational Behavior at Stanford University's Graduate School of Business, teaching your subordinates how to think and ask the right questions could be your most important task as a leader.

Avoid comparing team members with each other, as each person has unique traits and qualities. They do not all have the same speed, ability, or IQ level. Everyone operates on a different plane. Take that into consideration. Some subordinates may require motivation and a favorable isposition from you, while others may not need motivation. Take time to tudy their temperament, as it goes a long way in the delegation process.

ips for Delegating Tasks

)elegate Promptly

Learn to delegate assignments early enough to avoid unnecessary ressure. Give reasonable timelines for the execution of projects. Time onstraints and the eagerness to beat deadlines can result in low-quality erformance or errors with the project. As a manager, recognizing a project neant for delegation is a skill to learn. It will help you save time on not ttending to the tasks or waiting to delegate.

ears of Experience and Qualification Can Help You Decide How to)elegate

In assigning tasks, individual skills, talents and personality, years of xperience, expertise, academic qualification, and professional experience an help. People with various backgrounds can add more value to a project han relying on your capabilities or expertise alone.

3e Explicit With Context and Direction

Don't just hand over the task and expect them to figure it out. An dequately given guideline containing the functions and expectations will ;o a long way. It is always advisable for the team to work with documented erms of reference, by which they can hold each other accountable. Ensure hat the team lead communicates their plans (a report) back to you to be sure hey have everything correct before they forge ahead. Ambiguity in instruction might lead to erroneous execution of projects, waste o resources, and time.

Make Them Fully Responsible

All chains of command should be fully understood to help the tear work efficiently. Some projects might require access to funds, logistics, an other resources. Always let the team know who they can speak with to ge these things. Make sure the team can have access to the communicatio channel in case of issues. If you aren't there, assign someone to receiv reports and to take action for urgent matters. In all you do, let the team d their groundwork and take the initiative for their daily operations withou interference.

Create a Feedback Channel

As an addendum to the process, allowing open communication in th course of the project promotes increased productivity. Create time for th team and appreciate the efforts of subordinates by putting a feedbacl mechanism in place to make delegation an easy tool in the future. Feedbacl helps you know how each person feels about the projects, the team, an other issues. It will help you glean useful information to make the worl process better for the future. Also, if there is any vital information that wa left out or overlooked for any reason, feedback can help capture sucl details. Some people do not express their views better in a team. Usin feedback forms, surveys, and more, you can learn one or two truths fron reserved team members. When it is time to criticize a person's work o operational process, do so constructively and without prejudice. Criticisn should help correct and be used to take the right course, rather than to condemn. Therefore, criticism should focus on activities, not individuals.

Ensure you get a response on how comfortable it was to execute the task. You can also assess your performance as a manager in terms of assigning tasks, clarity of giving out instruction, ability to provide support for the team, and more. Armed with a comprehensive feedback system, you can also get useful plans and strategies for delegating projects.

Show Personal Interest in the Progress of the Work

Try not to be intrusive, but to request updates and give your perspective where necessary. In a case where performance appears below standard, don't take back the task. Provide as much support as you can and ensure they have a better understanding.

No individual has a monopoly on knowledge; therefore, even your subordinates should have the freedom to share ideas with you. You sometimes gain better perspectives from those you least expect. As each person strives to become better in their skills, you must invest in learning resources to lead or delegate better.

Effective delegation works better when you can help other team members grow on the job, develop the right skills, and take charge in turns. Delegation is about authority, responsibility, and accountability. Leaders must learn to use delegation to everyone's advantage, employee motivation, growth, and development.

Chapter Summary

- Delegation is a skill everyone needs to learn, particularly managers.

- The ability to delegate will determine how much success an organization or individual can enjoy. Delegation is utilizing several people's efforts to get tasks done, instead of allowing one person to get everything done.

- It saves time and allocates enough time for other responsibilities.

- Delegation reduces the workload of managers and allows them to make essential inputs.

- Putting aside all misconceptions about delegation will enable you to forge ahead.

- Delegation does not mean relegating your authority to others.

- When managers delegate, they multiply their effort, dividing it amongst their subordinates.

- It gives enough room to plan and strategize on more critical goals.

- The decision-making skills of the managers will improve the more they delegate.

- Delegation quickly results in business expansion and growth.

- It allows subordinates to identify and hone their skills.

- Delegation should follow a well-structured process.

- Decide on the duties to be delegated, determine who gets what, and put time factor into consideration.

- Give delegates ample opportunity to figure things out for themselves.

- Avoid micromanaging the team; it is the opposite of delegation.

- Providing an effective feedback mechanism in place will ensure things work better for the team, as well as to help you gain insight into challenges and successes in the group.

- When there is open communication, the workflow becomes smooth.

FINAL WORDS

It's been an exciting adventure, taking you through some of the most valuable productivity hacks available today. If you have come this far, taking your time to go through this book, then I dare say you mean business. If you put to practice most of what you have learned here, the difference in your productivity level should be evident in a matter of weeks. Also, within the space of 365 days, there should be an exponential growth in your achievements.

However, just to jostle your mind a bit, within the space of ten chapters, this book has looked at ten critical areas that will shape your future. By now, you can clearly outline the problems or issues confronting you in terms of your productivity. There are three key issues we addressed in this book that have to do with your productivity. First, the ability to draw up a workable plan that will help you to achieve your goals in life; second, the ability to focus your energy—it is best if you focus on critical things that will enhance your success in life—and third, your ability to stop the habits that can kill your productivity and develop the habits that will see you accomplish the life you have always dreamed of.

Having identified these three key issues, *Supercharge Productivity Habits* has provided the following time-tested solutions, or hacks, to help you become more efficient, productive, and a top performer in your industry. Central to your success are these three abridged solutions this book recommends:

The Need for a Workable Plan

It helps to have a plan to achieve your goals. That's one fact that this book has established. Having a plan in your head is no plan at all, as you cannot measure input and output effectively. To make your plan work effectively, you must first have a clear understanding of what you want out of life.

Your purpose will help you develop a workable plan of action. Focus your goals around your purpose. You are likely to be more successful and passionate in the areas in line with your purpose. Also, it will help if you have the right beliefs, develop the right habits, and shun negative beliefs. In addition, when setting goals, they should be SMART—Specific, Measurable, Achievable, Realistic, and Time-bound.

Focus Your Energy on Being Productive by Using Tools That Enhance Your Efficiency

Your success rating will depend on so many factors, but the first thing to consider is that you must act now. Procrastination is one of the major obstacles stopping people from pursuing and achieving their goals.

Robin Sharma's 5 A.M. Club provides an excellent tool for enhancing your productivity. Using the early hours of the morning, plan your day using his 20/20/20 principle. That means you spend the first 20 minutes exercising or meditating. The second 20 minutes should be used as a strategy session to plan your day. Then, the last 20 minutes should go into developing skills in an area that will help you achieve your one big goal.

Another exceptional tool this book looked at was the Personal Kanban planner and whiteboard. The Personal Kanban works by helping you to prioritize your tasks to focus on what's most important. It is made up of three columns. The first column is To-Do or Options, where you list all of your goals and tasks. The second column is Doing or the In-Progress column, where you place the tasks you want to work on now. The third column is the Done column, where you place the tasks you have completed. Having these details on your Personal Kanban whiteboard will help you to focus your energy on meaningful goals, pursue them, and complete more tasks at a faster rate.

With the Personal Kanban, you visualize your work when planning. Visualizing helps you see how the tasks can play out and helps to spur interest and excitement to start and finish them. The second principle of Personal Kanban is limiting your work progress. It involves starting and finishing a task before moving on to another one.

The TEA principle of Time, Energy, and Attention can help you fulfill your potential. However, some people only have two of these three attributes, hence they are not productive.

When you have energy, attention, and no time, you feel overwhelmed. People such as this have lots of energy and also pay attention to the most important tasks, but may feel out of time to complete them due to poor planning or procrastination.

153

Other people know how to manage their time and can pay attention, but lack the energy to get tasks completed. In cases such as these, a lack of energy often leads to frustration. However, eating right, sleeping well, exercising, and breaking tasks into smaller chunks, will help them to do better.

The third category of people have enough time and energy, but have a problem paying attention. These people are easily confused and overwhelmed. Whatever you do, you need the right dose of motivation to achieve success. Using science-backed tricks, like the high power pose, can help you to keep your motivation levels up.

To help increase your efficiency and focus further, the Pomodoro method can come in handy. Instead of spending 3 to 4 hours working at different tasks with little results, you can focus on a single task for 25 minutes and then take a 5-minute break. Doing this in intervals of 25 minutes and 5 minutes all through the workday can help you to get more done.

Kill the Habits That Can Kill Your Productivity

In the course of this book, I have identified several productivity killers and what you should replace them with.

- Replace multitasking with mono or single-tasking.

- Replace procrastination with action, doing it now (two-minute principle).

- Instead of working alone or trying to get things done alone, delegating tasks to others will help you to get more done faster and more efficiently.

So, What Next?

Take this book as a personal guide or companion. The truths learned here can last you a lifetime. One of the best ways to keep improving in what you have learned is to have *Supercharge Productivity Habits* as a reference book.

Put What You've Learned Into Practice

The investment in resources and time outlined in this book can only pay off once you take action with what you have learned. With the aid of tools like the Personal Kanban whiteboard, Robin Sharma's 20/20/20 rule, the 80/20 or Pareto principle, the TEA strategy for productivity, and the Pomodoro method, you are sure to become a top performer. All you have to do is put them to work.

Get an Accountability Buddy

One of the best ways to help yourself achieve your goals faster is to have someone to hold you accountable for setting them. Let your accountability partner know what goals you have decided to achieve and have them hold you up to it.

Build Teams

If you are a team lead, manager, or chief executive, the best way to increase your overall productivity is when other members of your team have access to the tools that help you. With this in mind, to help you rise faster, create a learning session with other members or staff to implement some of the strategies you have learned.

My Final Gift to You

If there is only one thing you can take away from this book, then I want it to be this fact: to be a top performer in any discipline, you must commit to a clearly defined plan of action. That action must be backed by the right beliefs, laced with discipline, and achieved one step at a time.

Success does not come from trying to do everything but in ensuring that the one thing you do, you do it right.

YOUR FREE GIFT

Thank you again for purchasing this book. As an additional thank you, you will receive an e-book, as a gift, and completely free.

This includes a fun and interactive daily checklist and workbook to help boost your productivity through simple activities. Life can get so busy, and this bonus booklet gives you easy and efficient tips and prompts to help you get more done, every day.

You can get the bonus booklet as follows:

To access the secret download page, open a browser window on your computer or smartphone and enter: **bonus.john-r-torrance.com**

You will be automatically directed to the download page.

Please note that this bonus booklet may be only available for download for a limited time.

RESOURCES PAGE

15 Ways to Boost Mental Energy Levels. (n.d.). Retrieved December 19, 2019, from https://www.faisonopc.com/office-supply-blog/boost-mental-energy-levels

10016 Therapists, Psychologists, Counseling - Therapist 10016 - Psychologist 10016. (n.d.). Retrieved December 19, 2019, from https://www.psychologytoday.com/us/therapists/10016?profid =318497&search=hershenson&ref=2&sid=1488894923.8327_ 24335&name=hershenson&tr=ResultsRow

admin. (2019, April 16). SMART Goals: Tips for Goal Setting. Retrieved December 19, 2019, from https://www.performancecoachuniversity.com/smart-goals-tips-for-goal-setting/

Alexander, L. (n.d.). How to Write a SMART Goal [+ Free SMART Goal Template]. Retrieved December 19, 2019, from https://blog.hubspot.com/marketing/how-to-write-a-smart-goal-template

American Psychology Association. (2010, April 5). Psychology of Procrastination: Why People Put Off Important Tasks Until the Last Minute. Retrieved December 19, 2019, from https://www.apa.org/news/press/releases/2010/04/procrastinati on

Baer, D. (2016, May 29). Why You Need To Unplug Every 90 Minutes. Retrieved December 19, 2019, from https://www.fastcompany.com/3013188/why-you-need-to-unplug-every-90-minutes

Benefits of Exercise. (n.d.-a). Retrieved December 19, 2019, from https://medlineplus.gov/benefitsofexercise.html

Benefits of Exercise. (n.d.-b). Retrieved December 19, 2019, from https://medlineplus.gov/benefitsofexercise.html

Benefits of Exercise. (n.d.-c). Retrieved December 19, 2019, from https://medlineplus.gov/benefitsofexercise.html

Benefits of Exercise. (n.d.-d). Retrieved December 19, 2019, from https://medlineplus.gov/benefitsofexercise.html

Berkeley University of California. (2019, August 13). The Impact of Ventilation on Productivity. Retrieved December 19, 2019, from https://cbe.berkeley.edu/research/impact-ventilation-productivity/

Bradberry, T. (2015, January 20). Multitasking Damages Your Brain And Career, New Studies Suggest. Retrieved December 19, 2019, from https://www.forbes.com/sites/travisbradberry/2014/10/08/multitasking-damages-your-brain-and-career-new-studies-suggest/#3dfdd3f956ee

Brain scans reveal "gray matter" differences in media multitaskers. (2014, September 24). Retrieved December 19, 2019, from https://www.eurekalert.org/pub_releases/2014-09/uos-bsr092314.php

Branson, R. (2010, September 17). Richard Branson On the Business of Life. Retrieved December 19, 2019, from https://www.americanexpress.com/en-us/business/trends-and-insights/articles/on-the-business-of-life-1/?linknav=us-openforum-search-article-link2

Cambridge Dictionary. (2019, December 18). prioritize definition: 1. to decide which of a group of things are the most important so that you can deal with them.... Learn more. Retrieved December 19, 2019, from https://dictionary.cambridge.org/dictionary/english/prioritize

Chu, M. (2018, May 17). Research Shows Listening to Music Increases Productivity (and Some Types of Music Are Super Effective). Retrieved December 19, 2019, from https://www.inc.com/melissa-chu/research-shows-listening-to-music-increases-produc.html

Clear, J. (2013, June 6). How to Stop Procrastinating and Stick to Good Habits by Using the "2-Minute Rule." Retrieved December 19, 2019, from https://www.lifehack.org/articles/productivity/how-stop-procrastinating-and-stick-good-habits-using-the-2-minute-rule.html

Conti, G. (2019, October 23). How to Delegate Tasks Effectively (and
Why It's Important). Retrieved December 19, 2019, from
https://www.meistertask.com/blog/delegate-tasks-effectively/

Corliss, J. (2019, August 5). Mindfulness meditation may ease anxiety,
mental stress. Retrieved December 19, 2019, from
https://www.health.harvard.edu/blog/mindfulness-meditation-
may-ease-anxiety-mental-stress-201401086967

Coscarelli, J. (2012, March 2). 63 Minutes With Jack Dorsey. Retrieved
December 19, 2019, from
http://nymag.com/news/intelligencer/encounter/jack-dorsey-
2012-3/

Cuddy, A. (n.d.). Your body language may shape who you are. Retrieved
December 19, 2019, from
https://www.ted.com/talks/amy_cuddy_your_body_language_
may_shape_who_you_are

Darius Foroux. (2019, October 29). The Pomodoro Method: Take
Strategic Breaks To Improve Productivity. Retrieved
December 19, 2019, from https://dariusforoux.com/takebreaks-
pomodoro/

Depression. (n.d.). Retrieved December 19, 2019, from
https://medlineplus.gov/depression.html

Don't read my lips! Body language trumps the face for conveying intense
emotions. (2013, January 15). Retrieved December 19, 2019,
from https://www.princeton.edu/news/2013/01/15/dont-read-

my-lips-body-language-trumps-face-conveying-intense-emotions?section=science

Dowling, T. (2017, November 25). What time do top CEOs wake up? Retrieved December 19, 2019, from https://www.theguardian.com/money/2013/apr/01/what-time-ceos-start-day

Economy, P. (2018, May 17). This Is the Way You Need to Write Down Your Goals for Faster Success. Retrieved December 19, 2019, from https://www.inc.com/peter-economy/this-is-way-you-need-to-write-down-your-goals-for-faster-success.html

Facebook COO Sheryl Sandberg talks personal tech. (2011, October 3). Retrieved December 19, 2019, from https://usatoday30.usatoday.com/tech/columnist/talkingyourtech/story/2011-10-03/talking-your-tech-sheryl-sandberg-facebook/50641034/1

Foods for change and motivation | Jean Hailes. (n.d.). Retrieved December 19, 2019, from https://jeanhailes.org.au/news/foods-for-change-and-motivation

Golemanova, R. (2019, October 15). 4 Easy Steps To More Successful Delegation. Retrieved December 19, 2019, from https://blog.hubstaff.com/delegate-tasks/

Grimsley, S. (2015, December 18). Delegation in Management: Definition & Explanation. Retrieved December 19, 2019, from https://study.com/academy/lesson/delegation-in-management-definition-lesson-quiz.html

Hartmans, A. (2018, May 7). How to dress like a tech billionaire for $200 or less. Retrieved December 19, 2019, from https://www.businessinsider.com/clothes-worn-by-tech-billionaires-2018-5?IR=T

Harvard Health Publishing. (2019, August 1). How much sleep do we really need? Retrieved December 19, 2019, from https://www.health.harvard.edu/staying-healthy/how-much-sleep-do-we-really-need

Hess, A. (2018, May 17). 10 highly successful people who wake up before 6 a.m. Retrieved December 19, 2019, from https://www.cnbc.com/2018/05/17/10-highly-successful-people-who-wake-up-before-6-a-m.html

How Lighting Affects the Productivity of Your Workers - Blog | MBA@UNC. (2017, September 11). Retrieved December 19, 2019, from https://onlinemba.unc.edu/blog/how-lighting-affects-productivity/

Introducing the Eisenhower Matrix. (n.d.). Retrieved December 19, 2019, from https://www.eisenhower.me/eisenhower-matrix/

Jack Dorsey LIVE Chat on. (2015, December 22). Retrieved December 19, 2019, from https://www.producthunt.com/live/jack-dorsey#comment-202183

Knapp, A. (2011, August 9). Meditation Leads to Greater Pain Relief Than Morphine. Retrieved December 19, 2019, from https://www.forbes.com/sites/alexknapp/2011/04/07/meditation -leads-to-greater-pain-relief-than-morphine/

Kosner, A. W. (2014, January 6). Why The Best Time To Drink Coffee Is Not First Thing In The Morning. Retrieved December 19, 2019, from https://www.forbes.com/sites/anthonykosner/2014/01/05/why-the-best-time-to-drink-coffee-is-not-first-thing-in-the-morning/#ba25f357a717

Laliberte, M. (n.d.). How to Be More Productive In Your First Hour of Work. Retrieved December 19, 2019, from https://www.rd.com/advice/work-career/productive-first-hour-work/1/

Lung Institute. (2017, January 27). Oxygen Levels and Brain Function. Retrieved December 19, 2019, from https://lunginstitute.com/blog/oxygen-levels-brain-function/

Manson, M. (2019, December 17). 7 Strange Questions That Help You Find Your Life... Retrieved December 19, 2019, from https://markmanson.net/life-purpose#footnote-2

Martin, G. (n.d.). "Procrastination is the thief of time" - the meaning and origin of this phrase. Retrieved December 19, 2019, from https://www.phrases.org.uk/meanings/procrastination-is-the-thief-of-time.html

McCall MD, T. (2017, April 12). 38 Health Benefits of Yoga. Retrieved December 19, 2019, from https://www.yogajournal.com/lifestyle/count-yoga-38-ways-yoga-keeps-fit

Murphy, M. (2018, April 15). Neuroscience Explains Why You Need To Write Down Your Goals If You Actually Want To Achieve Them. Retrieved December 19, 2019, from https://www.forbes.com/sites/markmurphy/2018/04/15/neurosc ience-explains-why-you-need-to-write-down-your-goals-if-you-actually-want-to-achieve-them/#5c06091e7905

NPR Choice page. (2008, August 21). Retrieved December 19, 2019, from https://choice.npr.org/index.html?origin=https://www.npr.org/2 008/08/21/93796200/to-lower-blood-pressure-open-up-and-say-om

Pardon Our Interruption. (n.d.). Retrieved December 19, 2019, from https://www.apa.org/research/action/multitask

Pink, D. (n.d.). The puzzle of motivation. Retrieved December 19, 2019, from https://www.ted.com/talks/dan_pink_the_puzzle_of_motivatio n?

Pochepan, J. (2019, February 19). This Aspect of Office Design Subtly Influences Employee Behavior. Retrieved December 19, 2019, from https://www.inc.com/jeff-pochepan/use-psychology-of-color-to-influence-your-work-day.html pubmeddev. (n.d.). A pilot study of yogic meditation for family dementia caregivers with depressive symptoms: effects on mental health, cognition, and telomerase acti... - PubMed - NCBI. Retrieved December 19, 2019, from https://www.ncbi.nlm.nih.gov/pubmed/22407663

Rampton, J. (2017, August 18). 15 Scientifically Proven Ways to Work Smarter, Not Just More. Retrieved December 19, 2019, from https://www.entrepreneur.com/article/298941

Robin Sharma | Official Website of the #1 Bestselling Author. (n.d.). Retrieved December 19, 2019, from https://www.robinsharma.com/

Schmitz, M. (2018, December 21). The 3 Pillars of Productivity You Need To Unlock Your Full Potential. Retrieved December 19, 2019, from http://www.asianefficiency.com/productivity/tea-framework/

Shandrow, K. L. (2015, March 9). How the Color of Your Office Impacts Productivity (Infographic). Retrieved December 19, 2019, from https://www.entrepreneur.com/article/243749

S.J. Scott. (2019, December 5). How to Get More Energy: 20 Tips to Boost Your Energy and Get More Done. Retrieved December 19, 2019, from https://www.developgoodhabits.com/get-more-energy/

Soojung-Kim Pang, A. (2017, May 9). Why you should work 4 hours a day, according to science. Retrieved December 19, 2019, from https://theweek.com/articles/696644/why-should-work-4-hours-day-according-science

Sorkin, A. R. (2014, September 6). So Bill Gates Has This Idea for a History Class ... Retrieved December 19, 2019, from https://www.nytimes.com/2014/09/07/magazine/so-bill-gates-has-this-idea-for-a-history-class.html?_r=0

Tadeo, M. (2014, November 8). Mark Zuckerberg on why he wears that same T-shirt every day. Retrieved December 19, 2019, from https://www.independent.co.uk/news/business/news/mark-zuckerberg-i-dont-like-spending-time-on-frivolous-decisions-such-as-clothes-or-what-to-make-for-9846827.html

The Bionic Manager - September 19, 2005. (2005, September 19). Retrieved December 19, 2019, from https://money.cnn.com/magazines/fortune/fortune_archive/2005/09/19/8272899/index.htm

To Multitask or Not to Multitask. (2018, July 17). Retrieved December 19, 2019, from https://appliedpsychologydegree.usc.edu/blog/to-multitask-or-not-to-multitask/

Valentine, M. (2019, September 25). 7 Habits to Increase Your Physical and Mental Energy. Retrieved December 19, 2019, from https://www.goalcast.com/2018/12/19/habits-increase-physical-mental-energy/

Walden University. (2019, May 16). 5 Mental Benefits of Exercise | Walden University. Retrieved December 19, 2019, from https://www.waldenu.edu/online-bachelors-programs/bs-in-psychology/resource/five-mental-benefits-of-exercise

Wang, D. (2018, September 7). 5 Surprising Tips To Increase Your Motivation Immediately. Retrieved December 19, 2019, from https://open.buffer.com/increase-your-motivation-tips/

Wertz, J. (2019, July 1). Open-Plan Work Spaces Lower Productivity And Employee Morale. Retrieved December 19, 2019, from https://www.forbes.com/sites/jiawertz/2019/06/30/open-plan-work-spaces-lower-productivity-employee-morale/#5d2f826761cd

What Is SMART and How Do I Write SMART Goals? (2019, July 3). Retrieved December 19, 2019, from https://www.thoughtco.com/how-do-i-write-smart-goals-31493

Why People Procrastinate: The Psychology and Causes of Procrastination. (n.d.). Retrieved December 19, 2019, from https://solvingprocrastination.com/why-people-procrastinate/

Wikipedia contributors. (2019, November 4). A picture is worth a thousand words. Retrieved December 19, 2019, from https://en.wikipedia.org/wiki/A_picture_is_worth_a_thousand_words#cite_note-1

Wong, K. (2016, December 9). The Case for Silence While You Work or Study. Retrieved December 19, 2019, from https://lifehacker.com/the-case-for-silence-while-you-work-or-study-1789847745

South American Bike ride June 2025 - Dec 2025

Voyage Dec 2025.

Printed in Great Britain
by Amazon